BUCOLIA:
Hijinx in the Hinterlands

By Matthew Thuney

Illustrations by Ellen Clark

ISBN-13: 978-1519400222

ISBN-10: 1519400225

DEDICATION

For my wife Donna, who brought me to Bucolia and continues to sow my life with seeds of joy, love, and wonder each and every day.

CONTENTS

ACKNOWLEDGMENTS

So many kind people helped see this book from seedling to blossom, that it would likely require another book to thank them all. Come to think of it, that's not a bad idea for a sequel. But for now, here's a very short list of *Bucolia's* best buddies: First of all, as you will soon discover, it is Ellen Clark's incredible illustrations that breathe life into my words and invite them to dance. I don't know how she managed to capture in images the spirit behind the thoughts, but she did. Perfectly. Ellen rendered the process of collaboration both fun and fruitful. Sort of like growing zucchini.

Thanks both literary and literal to fellow authors (I'm not sure I feel entirely comfortable including myself in their company yet) Chelsea Campbell and Charles Dickinson for responding to my often inane queries with sage advice. Which I parsley took most of the thyme. They always rose merry to the challenge. And now I'm certain they regret it. Nonetheless, if you haven't perused the works of Chelsea and Charles, do so immediately.

My humblest expressions of gratitude are reserved for the citizens of Bucolia—human, animal, and plant alike—who took me under their arms, wings, and branches and gave new meaning to my existence. A more welcoming, if sometimes challenging, group of critters than I could ever have hoped to meet in any place at any time.

And finally, thank you to all those inexplicably loyal readers who have followed my scribbling over the years and almost always approached me with a compliment (almost) and a question: "So, what are you up to these days?" Now you know.

i

Chapter 1: *In Which the Reader Is Introduced to Bucolia*

I know what you're wondering...just exactly what is this place called Bucolia, and where might we find it?

Bucolia is a place, maybe like your town or that quaint little hamlet out by the foothills an hour's drive down the highway, where friends come to meet old friends and make new ones; a place you just wind up in, not quite realizing why you were headed that way or how you got there.

It's a place where, if there are any "corner stores" at all, they're roughly 2.7 miles away. But you're sure to find a friendly face behind the counter, and some of the strangest, most exotic, wonderful homespun creations and concoctions on the shelves.

It's a place where you're as likely to see cows, deer, rabbits, possums, and raccoons on the road as you are to see Tauruses, Tundras, Thunderbirds, or Tacomas. Well, maybe a vintage Thunderbird from the Sixties, but that'll be well off the road in some fellow's barn waiting on a rebuilt motor.

And if there's a jam on the road, it's probably caused by a tractor, not traffic.

And "distracted driving" isn't caused by your infatuation with some high-falutin' electronic device; it's on account of you're keeping a wary eye on that load of hay you're toting or horse trailer you've got hitched to your rig.

And the roadsides are not cluttered with gas stations and mini-malls, but dotted with makeshift wooden flower and vegetable stands, honey and egg booths where you can pick up fresh produce...just leave your money in the pickle jar.

In Bucolia, folks tend to communicate more over their fence posts and on their front porches than they do by pressing buttons on a piece of high-tech plastic. It's an old method of communication called "talking" or "conversing," and it seems to work pretty well when it comes to catching up on news or, especially, gossip.

In Bucolia, neighbors who might be divided every couple of years by the political signs stuck in their front yards are united year-round at block parties, picnics, potlucks, barn dances, and places of fellowship—whether those be holy sanctuaries or mountain meadows.

In Bucolia, spectacular sunrises and sunsets are framed by rolling hills, magnificent mountains, flowing fields of grain; instead of being hemmed in by clustered condos, reflected off shiny towers of steel or obscured by hazy hillside office complexes.

At night in Bucolia, the wailing you hear won't come from sirens, but from the mournful horn of a rumbling freight train with the coyotes serenading its passage. Or maybe the woodland owls. Perhaps even the occasional howling Sasquatch.

There's nothing like the smell of fresh-mown fields in Bucolia. Or the smell of fields freshly spread with manure. On opposite ends of the olfactory spectrum mind you.

In Bucolia, we consider any town with a supermarket or more than one gas station The Big City.

Bucolia is a cozy home to rest your weary bones after a hard day's work, a haven to refresh your weary soul when worldly troubles threaten to wear you down.

Bucolia leads you to hope that, when at long last you pass from this world, your next destination will be a little like the place you're leaving. Perhaps without the aforementioned manure.

Long story short: you most likely won't find Bucolia on any map— even Google maps—but you might just be able to locate it as a place in your heart. I know it has a place in mine, and I'm so honored and pleased to have you join me here, even if only for a little while.

"So now you know," as my sister-in-law is wont to say when she's trying desperately to tell me something I don't quite get. Or maybe don't want to. But how did I come to dwell in Bucolia, what have I discovered here and why might you want to visit? Well, let's do something that I very rarely do, which is begin at the beginning with my first meager musings about the place I now call home...

Bucolic.

That's where we live now. No wait, that's *how* we live now. That's not right, either. Lemme see...bucolic, adjective, meaning pastoral, rural, rustic. So you might say we live in a bucolic fashion, paradigmatically speaking, encompassed by bucolic views in a vivaciously bucolic valley, surrounded by bucolic cows and horses, visited by the occasional not-so-bucolic coyote and gray wolf, enjoying a decidedly bucolic...

Let's just say we live in the damn country now. I simply fell in love with the word bucolic. So there you have it, my first confession of many.

How about this: hereafter, the town into which my wife and I recently moved shall be known as Bucolia.

Actually, my wife grew up here. I reckon that's confession #2. Me? I've almost always been a city boy, though comfortable in suburban confines as well. But this country thing? It's new to me. Sort of like the *plantar fasciitis* I now suffer from due to stomping on shovels so doggone much. My heels ache and my arches don't arch like they used to. Hello, country living. We'd better be blessed with a whole lot of gorgeous flowers and tasty vegetables or yours truly will be one pissed-off and sore-footed city mouse.

So welcome to our journey. As I write this, I can see cattle grazing outside my office window, my wife hoeing gamely away at a bunch of sod and weeds we hope someday to call a garden, and—oh, look!— it's beginning to rain…hard…again. Hi, honey! She's waving back at me. Not quite a wave, really. Only one finger involved. She appears to be heading back indoors. She announces she's done gardening for the night. Coward! Just when I was about to go out and join her, too.

Time to retreat to kitchen and living room. As long as we have electricity (always a gamble here), there's dinner (or is it supper…more about that later) to cook and TV shows about cops, impending financial/social/political doom, more cops, close encounters with alien creatures of questionable moral fiber, android cops, scary ghosts, and Seattle Mariner games (equally spooky) to watch.

Or *Bonanza* reruns. They're starting to look pretty good. And realistic.

And, truth be told, I've fallen as much in love with country life as I have with the word bucolic. It just seems like you ought to cough 'em both up every now and then.

Matthew Thuney

Chapter 2: *In Which Matt Seeks Help for His Disgusting, Deranged Addiction*

Here at Planters Anonymous, we start our meetings with a simple prayer:

"Goddess, grant us the strength to plant that which will be pleasing to You, the courage to dig up that which does not belong, and the wisdom to differentiate hawkweed from hydrangea."

Then, following a period of sharing tales of transplanting terror, comparing of calluses, and grieving over sickly shrubs and lost herbs (our pet basil succumbed after a brief frost last week), our meetings generally conclude with an impromptu *ceilidh* and several bottles of Merlot.

I mention all this as prelude to confession #3: My name is Matthew, and I am a serial digger. I wasn't always this way, mind you. I used to spend my spare time in innocent inactivities such as reading, writing (if that's what you call this), napping, and—equally exciting— watching the Seattle Mariners lose on TV. But not now.

Now that we've moved to the country, I've begun planting things. And I can't seem to stop. Even today, with rain pouring down (such a surprise in the Pacific Northwest), I'm itching to sally forth into our vegetable-garden-turned-bog and plant the tomato starts we purchased yesterday. But no, such madness would not be pleasing to the Goddess, would it? Although it would definitely be pleasing to my doctor, as my annual bouts with colds, flu and lung infections no doubt help pay his greens fees at the local country club. Whenever he senses me sniffling, I'm certain he grabs the phone and reserves a tee time.

It began benignly enough: we asked our friends to bring plants as gifts to our housewarming party. As it turns out, that was like inviting high rollers to Caesar's for craps. Like gamblers and Vegas, the plants and I just couldn't get enough of each other. And, as you can see, I now share their codependent madness. I'm even prone to betting the field as I garden. What next? Will I, too, turn against my own best interest? Start digging up the very veggies and flowers that would sustain my life and well-being, only to sow something ugly and dysfunctional? Like beets? Or Brussels sprouts, for heaven's sake?

Just in order to continue the act of digging, like some crazed bone-burying puppy on a mission from the God of Dogs?

But no, I will not plant, if only for today. One day at a time, as they say.

After all, here in Bucolia there are indoor tasks to address. A little caulking to finish up, some touch-up painting, the obligatory dusting and vacuuming associated with new construction.

On the other hand, there's that Mariners game on the tube. What better way to escape reality and engage in self-flagellation for a couple of hours.

Speaking of which (reality, I mean, not flagellation—this is, after all, a G-rated—or perhaps PG—book), can anyone tell me where all the Sasquatch have gone? Since moving smack-dab into Sasquatch Suburbia, we've not heard a peep out of our mysterious neighbors. Have they simply shrugged, sighed "Here come the Thuneys; there goes the neighborhood," and moved out? Have they drowned in this incessant downpour? Have they been frightened off by my incessant digging?

Or are they simply hiding out, biding their time, licking their hairy chops, waiting for our bounteous harvest to burst forth, taking numbers for the forthcoming feast at our buffet?

Well bring it on, Mr. Sasquatch. I have a shovel. And I'm not afraid to use it.

Chapter 3: The Ark, or, The House that Came Over the Mountain

Part I: the Bridge

"Nothing is impossible." Someone once told me that. It may have been my grandmother. It may have been my high school physics or industrial arts teachers who did their damnedest to convince themselves that I could learn the secrets of wave theory or how to fashion a skateboard out of a simple plank of wood (hah…the woefully naïve fools!). Or it may have been my introductory philosophy professor at Texas Christian University, for whom the idea of nothingness was indeed impossible. Wow!

Nonetheless, I would submit to you that after listening to the following tale of woe and travail, you will agree that anything can be done. Absolutely anything.

When first we decided to move to this faraway hilly haven of Bucolia, my wife and I debated the possibilities of homesmanship. What kind of home would best suit our needs? What sort of structure would endure the wild wilderness weather? And, most importantly, what kind of humble hovel could we afford?

A conventional "stick-built" house? Quite the project, especially considering all the amenities and oddball living, office, and bedroom arrangements we dreamed of including. Architects, engineers, and teams of *feng shui* psychics might have to be consulted. This option was just too complex. Not to mention too pricey.

What about a log cabin? To be sure, that would perfectly complement our new rustic lifestyle way out in the woods. Kits are available, complete with blueprints chockablock with options for various configurations of living space. We began pricing these seemingly simplistic kits. Yikes! Then we began researching the amount of upkeep involved with a wood home. Double Yikes!! This option was also too pricey. And way, way too much upkeep.

Finally, we settled on a manufactured home. We were sore amazed (yes, for no apparent reason I just went all King-Jamesy in the midst of this hair-raising tale) by all the options available. You can switch a living room with a dining room, a bedroom with a study, add on a bathroom here, a utility room there, adjust the pitch of the roof, add windows and doors, stretch this, flip that, and voila! You have a custom-made home for not, well, relatively, not-so-much cash. And very little maintenance.

Goldilocks leapt for joy. This option was just right.

Except for one thing.

How to transport newly purchased, high-roofed, custom-designed manufactured home (a) to well-dug, electrically wired, septic-ready property (b).

You see, in order to get to our property from the nearest highway one must cross a river. And in order to cross that river one must come through a bridge. A very narrow, ancient, one-lane bridge. A very narrow, ancient one-lane bridge with metal girders on the sides…and on the top.

"Golly," my wife and I repeatedly cautioned the home sales staff, "We're not sure you can fit this humongous house through that tiny bridge."

At which point our construction contractor, who had just taken various precise laser measurements of said mini-bridge, chimed in, "Are you kidding me? There's no way you can fit *that* friggin' house through *that* friggin' bridge."

Was the manufactured home sales staff worried? Not for a moment. Besides, they were too deafened by the sound of our hard-earned coin tumbling into their bank account to be able to hear the warnings.

So the day gradually approached for the delivery of our home. And by "gradually" I mean that assembling our home on, say, the eastern coast of Russia and waiting for the process of continental drift to float the completed house to the Pacific Northwest would have been more expedient than the procedure employed by the home dealership.

For the next few months, merry little conversations like this dragged on and on: "Mr. Thuney, I have wonderful news. Your home will be delivered this coming Saturday!"

"You mean it'll fit through the bridge?"

"What bridge?"

"The small one-lane bridge we told you about."

"Oh, *THAT* bridge. Not a problem. See you Saturday."

Then came that fateful Saturday night: "Mr. Thuney, howya doin'? Apologies for not being able to deliver the home today, but rest assured our crew is on the way and Sunday's the day!"

"So, no problem with the bridge," I cautiously wondered.

"What bridge?"

I paused, took a deep breath, then calmly reiterated, "The small one-lane bridge we told you about. Our contractor gave you the dimensions."

"Oh, *THAT* bridge. We can tilt the home a little bit to the side and she'll slide right through."

And so it went. On, and on, and on…

Part II: The Long & Winding Logging Road

Then, some two weeks (which seemed more like two years) later: "Mr. Thuney, we're *SO* sorry about the delay in delivering your home. We've encountered one small problem. Were you aware there's a tiny one-lane bridge that we have to cross?"

I reached for the nearest roll of antacids, poured myself a shot of whiskey, then muttered, "Yes, we warned you repeatedly about that. So did our contractor."

"Well, it's not so much a problem as a challenge. You see, good buddy, we have the angle of tiltage for your home vis-à-vis said bridge all figured out. We just deflate the tires on the transport trailers, turn everything just so, and squeeze the whole works through on skids. We'll have your home in place next Tuesday. Trust me, old pal."

Three weeks later: "So here's what we'll do, Mr. Thuney. We're going to cut off the roof of the home, slide the main sections through the bridge, then reassemble all the pieces once they're on your property. Now, all the additional permits required for this reconstruction will take several weeks and may cost a few hundred dollars, but..."

"F**k you."

"Sorry?"

"You've been jerking us around for weeks now, promising this and that and spewing out definite delivery dates like year-old candy from a hemorrhaging three-legged piñata. I frankly can't believe a thing you say."

"Jerked around? Really, Mr. Thuney, we're doing our best to…oooh, look at that!"

"What now?"

"Mr. Thuney, I may have good news. As we speak, I'm looking at Google Earth on my monitor. There seems to be a logging road that reaches from a paved highway to your road beyond the alleged bridge!"

By this time, I'm suspecting that it's actually Alan Funt on the other end of the line and I've been transported back in time to a rerun of *Candid Camera*. I stealthily scan the room for one-way mirrors hiding secret film crews, while mumbling, "I'm sorry, did you say a *logging* road?"

"Yes! Oh, this looks promising indeed."

"Does Google Earth mention that there's a small mountain between that paved highway and the road to our property? And that, to get from there to here the logging road is primitive, narrow, and full of switchbacks?"

"Well, the path does look a bit squiggly to be sure, but not to worry, Mr. Thuney; I do believe we've found a way to deliver your home in no time at all. Hang in there, chum. I'll call you right back with the details." Click.

As you might guess, another week passed, filled with unanswered phone and email messages. My old pal acid reflux, unheard from in a couple of years, began scouring my stomach with renewed vigor. I couldn't sleep. I began cursing at impish children and small dogs. Finally, I fired off a rather succinct email to the parent company of our home dealership. The subject line read, *"Where the hell is our home?"* The text went downhill from there. It was one of the uglier emails I've ever sent.

Next day, I got a call from the dealership.

"Mr. Thuney, I heard from my boss late last night. Seems as though you're upset with our performance so far. I can understand that, buddy. But I'm here to tell you that your home is moving up the road to the paved highway and we'll be on the logging road tomorrow afternoon."

Part III: The Charge up the Mountain

To recap: months of delay, chicanery and general Monty Python-style perplexing machinations on behalf of the dealership that sold us our outsized manufactured home had elapsed, during which various schemes (ranging from laughably outrageous to certifiably insane) were entertained regarding how best—and apparently most dangerously-- to get the home from Point A (the dealership) to Point B (our property) avoiding the ultimate obstacle Point C (the tiny ancient steel-covered river bridge through which said home would most assuredly not fit). Giant cranes and military-grade helicopters were seriously considered to lift the home over the river, circumventing the bridge. When our dealership sobered up and was able to do the math, however, a crazed journey over a mountain logging road was deemed the best option.

Did I mention the Monty Python part?

So, when last we met, dear reader, Arthur, Lancelot, and Bedivere were all set to embark on the holy quest of transporting said domicile up over a tortuously twisted mountain logging road and down to our property. Or so they thought.

The dealership hired two Cats, one to pull each half of the home from the front, the other to guide it through various twists and turns from the rear. From what I understood at the time—being a soon-to-be-ex-urbanite—these cats were neither Persian nor Calico, but some sort of motorized, tractorized contraptions with treads. Wigged out as I was at this point from countless sleepless nights and a spectacular resurgence of acid reflux, I took solace in envisioning these gizmos as advancing Allied tanks, with Patton at the forefront shouting "On to Palermo, lads!" Not sure if Patton actually marched on Palermo, but for the purposes of this particular fever-pitched fantasy that suited just fine.

Then, shock of all shocks, another delay. Just as our charging phalanx of home and tanks approached the logging road's gates, the hot summer weather (of course we were blessed with a *real* summer that year) cooled, drizzle moistened the forest, and the logging company informed our home movers that they had been approved by the Department of Natural Resources to resume their tree-cutting activities on the very mountain our home was to traverse. Their deforestation business being considered a higher priority than our bizarre request to send a double-wide manufactured home over their road, the logging company kindly let us know that we'd just have to wait until they were finished sacking and pillaging that section of the mountain. Fortunately, like a stray gang of deviant locusts or a staggering drunk on Karaoke night, the logging company's savagery was short-lived, and after a week or so our intrepid squad was allowed through the gates and onto the road.

"We should have your home on the other side of the mountain by this afternoon," exclaimed our salesman triumphantly as he phoned us from the head of the charge up the hillside. I must confess to a tad bit of skepticism. Can't imagine why. After all, the dealership up to now had been as forthright with us as a meth-head courting a prom queen.

And so we waited eagerly all morning and into the early afternoon for word of Patton's progress as the squadron completed its mountain conquest. As evening fell along with our spirits, Donna and I finally received a weary phone call. "Well, it wasn't easy," sighed our salesman heavily into my earpiece, "but I can honestly tell you that your home is safe and sound."

"Oh, thank God, it's down on our property," I exhaled.

"Not exactly."

"How not exactly?"

"Your home is parked off to the side of the logging road, safe and sound, at the very top of the mountain."

"Say *what?*"

"As it turns out, the path downward is just a tidge steeper than we had anticipated. Now, we have every confidence that we can bring your home down the other side…"

"I'm sorry; did you say *the top of the mountain?*"

"…but we'll have to bring in some special equipment. Only take a day or two…"

"Our home is stuck at *the top of the mountain?* Hello?"

"…and I'll be in touch with you then. No worries, bro! We'll have your home down the mountain in a jiffy. Did I tell you how beautiful it looks inside? You and Donna made some excellent interior choices. Nice work! Talk to you soon!"

Part IV: Down at Last, Down at Last, Thank God Almighty, We Are Down at Last!

So for ten long, lonely days, that's where our two-part manufactured home sat, perched on the peak of a mountainous logging road. Delirious as I was from anger, frustration and a burgeoning desire to commit physical violence in creative and extensive ways upon the next spokesperson I encountered from our dealership, my mind began to wander. Even more than usual, that is.

While Donna and I stewed below and the movers tried to figure out a way to bring both huge halves of the home down the mountain, I began to wonder what fate might be befalling our future abode up at the summit. With each half being protected only by a sheet of vinyl, surely all sorts of woodland creatures must be creeping in at night, making themselves right at home in our living room, crashing out in our bedrooms, sacking my office, cooking up a mess of Sloppy Joes in our kitchen and tracking gooey sauce and grease all through our formal dining room. Who knew? Perhaps drunken poker games broke out regularly 'round midnight in our freshly minted living room, with genial camaraderie twixt Gray Wolf, Brown Bear, Raven and Sasquatch devolving into all-out brawls as the evening wore on, fueled by heated exchanges like this:

Raven (ever the trickster/cheater) as a fifth ace tumbles from under his wing: "Hey, Squatch, you mind cutting back on the salmon? And would it kill you to grab a bottle of Scope from the next campers you terrorize? Jeez, could your breath be any worse?"

Bear (carefully sharpening his claws on our newly painted walls): "Yeah, ya big ape. A bar of Irish Spring might come in handy, too."

Sasquatch (eying the assembled players with arched brow): "Begging your pardon, but I am NOT an ape. I happen to be a hominid, and you will excuse me if personal hygiene is not high on the list of my species' priorities. As interdimensional beings, we have larger concerns to consider. Besides, you, Mr. Raven, still have skunk in your teeth, and you, Mr. Bear, continually assail us with horrendous gaseous emissions as the result of an overzealous intake of Sloppy Joes. Meanwhile, speaking of interdimensional, has anyone bothered to notice that Mr. Gray Wolf has gone all-in with six-of-a-kind?'

Gray Wolf (whimpering, but in a menacing way): "Beats five aces, don't it? Hey, gimme me a break; I'm on the friggin' brink of extinction here!"

Eventually though, after a week and a half, the phone did ring. We were informed that the house movers had acquired some magical piece of machinery known as a "Jadde" from faraway Oregon. Said Jadde was allegedly capable of turning huge objects on the proverbial dime and so it did. One half of the home wriggled its way painstakingly down the mountain, then the other. It was then that I came to the amazing epiphany that miracles do happen. It's just that they're often caused by incredibly stupid people doing the exact opposite of what any reasonable human being might expect.

One last glitch: getting the home off the road and onto our property. Too lengthy for any known earthly machine to swing the bodies of the home from pavement, across culvert, through gate, onto destined bit of land, it was beginning to seem likely that Donna and I would be forced to set up housekeeping in the middle of the road, much to the consternation of our rural neighbors. I began thinking of the upside: We could place one half of the house in the left lane, the other in the right, place a tollgate in-between, and thereby help finance our mortgage payment.

Nevertheless, it was not to be. Another magical bit of machinery—this one remote-controlled by a simple joystick—was brought into play. Jockeying both halves of the house back and forth with video-game precision, the operator was able to maneuver our home into place with amazing ease.

An immense burden of aggravation began slowly lifting from my beleaguered shoulders as it dawned on me that 1) our house was indeed home where it belonged, and more importantly, 2) this particular delivery must've cost the dealership a record amount of money.

Once the Eagle had landed (that's a moon mission reference, for those of you too young to remember or too earthbound to care), we clambered inside the home and found to our immense surprise that the interior was laid out exactly as we had planned it. And, by all that's holy (and somewhat ain't), it was indeed a thing of great beauty.

Except for the cracked drywall. And the broken mirrors. And the dangling light fixtures. And the fractured ceilings. Well, you get the picture. For some strange reason, it looked as though this house had been dragged up one side of a mountain and down the other. Still, no claw marks or Sloppy Joe stains, which was a great relief.

Thus ended the saga of the House that came over the Mountain.

And thus began the Battle of the Hillside.

Matthew Thuney

Chapter 4: The Battle of the Hillside, or, Thank God I'm a Carnivore

Part I: Cattlegate

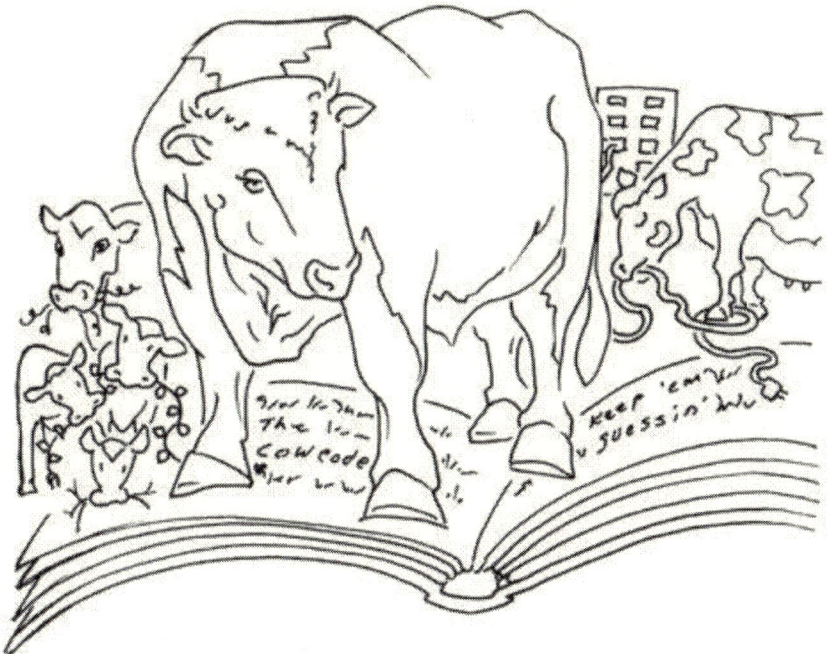

Cows. I hate 'em. Unless they're on my plate, that is. All nicely sliced up and cooked just so.

Now don't get me wrong, I haven't always been a charter member of the Anti-Bovine League. Fact is, like most folks, I used to be quite taken by the dewy-eyed, fat-lipped, barrel-chested buffoons. Until I uncovered their true purpose--to sow discord, mistrust and generally foul-smelling mayhem amongst us human beings.

How did I reach this admittedly controversial conclusion? Well, pull up a chair (preferably a leather one) while I let you in on the details of this grand cowspiracy...

The shouts of joy upon seeing our beloved new home safely ensconced on our property had barely finished echoing off the mountainsides when we were faced with our first challenge. Need I tell you that cows were involved?

You see, my wife Donna's dad—we'll call him "Vernon"—had been running cattle on the land since, well, since cattle were invented. We fully intended to allow him to continue said practice, given that he would fence off a good-sized lot around our home and allow us, in return, the grandiose concession of a driveway. Problem is, that driveway would stand squarely in the path that Vernon employed to herd his cows from one seasonal pasture to another. So, months before the torturous moving of the house over the mountain, Donna and I sat in her dad's kitchen drawing out plans for fencing, driveway and a gate to accommodate this bovine thruway.

Looking back, I should've been able to hear those blasted cows snickering and plotting right then and there.

For, lo and behold, no sooner had the home landed on the lot than Vernon (no doubt duped by his beloved beasts) decided to radically alter the gate arrangement so that our driveway would in effect cut straight through our front lawn. This, he insisted with a mad look of cowfusion in his eye, was the plan we had originally agreed upon and he would hear of no other. And, by "hear" of no other, I mean that literally. On account of—following years of work at sawmills and on tractors—Vernon is just a wee bit hard of hearing. And, by "wee bit," I mean a lot bit. When one has a conversation with Donna's dad, there's always a great deal of shouting involved, followed by many phrases like, "Eh," "What's that," or simply awkward silence. Generally speaking, what Vernon gets out of a conversation is whatever he came in wanting to hear. God love the man.

Which reminds me of an incident that occurred before the house came over the mountain when final site preparations were being made. Our contractor needed access to the property where Vernon's cattle were grazing and plotting their next move, so he phoned me upon arrival in order that I could in turn phone Vernon and ask him to open the gate. That phone call went something like this:

Vernon: "Hello?"

Me: "Hi Vernon, it's Matt."

V: "Hello? Hello?"

M: "It's me, Matt!"

V: "Who is this?"

M: "Matt!! You know, Matthew?"

V: "Who?"

M: "Matthew!! Your son in law, Matt? Matthew!!!"

V: "Oh. I love you, too."

M: "No! It's Matthew!! The contractor is at the gate!!! Can you go let him in, please?"

V: "What? The gate? Gate's locked."

M: "Yes! The gate! Could you go open the gate and let the contractor in?"

V: "Who is this?"

M: "It's Matthew!! Please go let…"

V: "I love you, too."

Perhaps you, like me, might wonder how it was so easy for an 82-year-old man to express his affection over the phone to someone he thought to be a complete stranger, but such are the conundrums that have now become part of daily life in our new home. Anyhow, now you have a taste of the type of insurmountable auditory odds that we were up against gate-wise.

So there we stood—Donna, Vernon and I—in the middle of our soon-to-be front yard, arguing vehemently about where gate and driveway would go. I tried loudly but in vain to remind Vernon of the layout in our original kitchen-table drawings. Nevertheless, he persisted in some sort of cow-inspired delusion involving multiple gates and a driveway that would bisect Donna's planned dahlia beds and totally trash her carefully laid out *feng shui* flow. I always simply smiled and nodded when she brought up the latter, assuming *feng shui* to be Chinese for "husband need not go there." Finally, Vernon walked away, crushed that his own daughter would side with her clearly crazed husband in thwarting his best-laid plans of cattle herding.

Just over a nearby rise I caught a glimpse of cows nodding knowingly, their eyes glistening with triumph.

I tried, in decibel levels rarely reached by the human voice, to assuage Vernon's fears about our assault upon his cattle trail, but to no avail. He was disconsolate. He might just have to quit the cattle game altogether and go live in a hovel in the city, leading a lonely existence where no one would come visit him and it would always be rainy, cold and bereft of the sweet smell of cow shit.

Days passed. Donna and I fretted. Had we overstepped our bounds? Perhaps the cows were right and we should surrender to their evil plot. Was it better to be cowed than cause an irreparable family rift?

Then, one day, Donna's dad called and asked us to meet him at the property. Good thing Donna answered the phone. They seem to understand each other just fine. And, by "fine" I mean somewhat. So, out to the hillside we drove and found Vernon standing in our proposed driveway clutching a drawing of a new proposal for the gate. Staring at the page, Donna and I glanced at each other in disbelief.

There, in Vernon's hand, was a virtual replica of our original kitchen-table plan. One gate. One dahlia-intact, Feng Shui-approved driveway.

Taking the drawing from Vernon, turning it this way and that, pausing for a few thoughtful "hmmm" and "oh, I see" breaks, I took my good time before returning it to Vernon and pronouncing (with great vigor), "You know, I think this just might work!!!!" Vernon grinned and shook my hand.

Across the field, the defeated bovine minions could be heard (by Donna and me, at least) lowing in dark dismay. We humans had emerged victorious from the first skirmish in the Battle of the Hillside.

Part II: Cowrilla Warfare

So the battle had been joined: Herefords vs. Humans, Cloven-Hoofed vs. Biped, Grazers vs. Squatters. For surely, Donna and I had imposed our home upon the pasture land of Vernon's vengeful bovine minions. However, as the superior species—at least in terms of mental capacity, manual dexterity, and the possession of various grilling implements—we were determined to assert our manifest destiny over these plotting, pooping apostates.

Admittedly, I should've seen it coming.

Just the year before, Donna and I had traveled out to the property in order to help with the annual cattle drive. It was a simple task of herding the cattle from one field to another across a two-lane road into the very space that would soon be occupied by our home. The cattle must've sensed the winds of change wafting across our bucolic valley, must've foreseen our evil plan to seize their beloved thruway and transform it into driveway and garden.

For, that year, this particular herd decided secretly to recruit a Hereford terrorist, a certain wily steer known only by the name Enrique. Masterminded by Enrique, the docile procession from field to field of years past was not to be. No, this psycho steer (doubtless a diligent student of radical teachings of the Qowran) was bent on preventing not only the safe passage of the herd, but on inflicting as much pain as bovinely possible upon the human herders.

Roaming wildly apart from his cohorts, Enrique snorted, ran, and leapt as Vernon, Donna, and I, accompanied by a phalanx of unwitting neighbors, closed in upon the cow clan. Spaced far apart and with our arms outstretched like great birds of prey, we puny humans attempted to assert our tenuous authority, outflanking the cattle and guiding them toward the desired gate.

But Enrique would have none of it. Mad-eyed and bucking like a rabid mule, he commanded his rebellious comrades to swerve, dodge and otherwise cowfound our attempts to lead them in the path of human righteousness.

Led by this nefarious steer, the cattle continued to circumvent our flanks, dancing around us with guerilla-style tactics and taunts that, after an hour or so, began to leave us worn down and despondent. Clearly, it was time to bring in the armored brigade.

Which was one of those little four-wheeled ATV's piloted by the farmer next door. At first, the results were impressive: as the ATV roared toward the cattle, they compressed into a small, bewildered bunch of cowed adversaries. However, Enrique, comprehending the limited nature of the threat, commanded his platoon simply to circle the fence line, back and forth, forth and back, waiting for our toothless tank to run out of fuel. Weary and worn from mucking around in the field for so long, we humans began to lose our taste for battle. Sensing this, Enrique decided to strike.

Without warning and ignoring our armored division altogether, Enrique struck at our weakest points. First, he charged a small woman on our left flank. Knocked her down, but then backed off triumphant awaiting our capitulation. When she popped right back up and we re-grouped, Enrique decided it was time to end this charade and take on the ringleader, the ancient one, he who has herded since time immemorial: Vernon.

Enrique charged. Vernon raised his arms and grunted with great gusto. Yet Enrique prevailed, as Vernon was toppled head over heels, his John Deere cap sent flying. Enrique eyed us all with a victorious glint, demanding immediate surrender. His minions, lowing Enrique's praises, began chanting "No more houses, no more gates! No more houses, no more gates!" Yet, gradually, and with a steadfastness borne of years of facing down contentious steers, Vernon regained his feet, stretched out his arms, and advanced slowly but surely upon Enrique.

"Way to go, Vern," I shouted, "that cow is plum loco!"

Now, in my own defense, I must admit that I'd always wanted to utter the phrase "plum loco" in a meaningful (i.e. agrarian/western) context. That lifelong wish being fulfilled, I now began to realize what Enrique's next move might be. Namely, attacking the truly weakest link in the human line of resistance.

Which would be me.

Before I knew it, Enrique was rumbling full-tilt toward me with a look of great glee as I backpedaled furiously in abject terror. What happened next was either, a) Enrique hit me full-force as I valiantly grabbed onto his ears and fought for mastery of the land, or, b) I tripped and stumbled over my own feet, falling ingloriously on my ass as Enrique looked on with pity in his winking eye and victory in his crooked grin. You can likely guess which.

So now the battle had raged nearly two hours. Discouraged and in disarray, we humans huddled together trying to decide what to do next. Some voted for running away; others for fighting another day. I straggled dazedly away in an attempt to find out what had happened to my beloved wife Donna.

I found her in a far corner of the field seemingly chatting amiably with the hated Enrique. What's this, I thought, has she gone over to the other side? But as I continued to stagger toward Donna, I noticed a peculiar thing: Enrique had rejoined his troop and the entire band was now heading slowly across the road toward the gate that opened onto the opposite field.

"You okay?" Donna asked as I shambled up to her, hat askew and covered in mud.

"Yep," I said a bit too shrilly, "That cow was plum loco! By the way, what just happened here?"

"Oh," said Donna casually, "I just asked him if he wasn't as tired as we were and wouldn't he like to lead his friends across to that tempting, tasty-looking field to have something good to eat."

"Huh," I offered with grand intelligence, watching the cattle plod indifferently through the long-contested gate and road.

Did I mention that Donna was raised on a farm? Her dad Vernon's farm, to be precise?

Did I mention I wasn't?

Part III: I Sing the Bovine Electric!

I'm going to let you in on a little secret. Come closer, we don't want this to reach the wrong ears, if you know what I mean. Let's just make a quick check of the immediate perimeter to certify that no stray cattle are wandering by. Their spies *are* everywhere, you know. Okay, the coast (or field) appears to be clear, so here goes...

Some cows? They just ain't natural. Something fishy going on, if you know what I mean. For instance, the cows that roam around our property? I have proof positive they are not human. Well, not bovine. Flesh and blood. Hide and udder. Steak and rump roast. Heck, you know what I mean.

Or do you?

Maybe you, like me, swallowed the bucolic myth that cattle are simply cute, dumb, occasionally ornery and brutish animals who are harmless (apart from their malodorous droppings) and good to eat.

Hah! That's what they'd *like* you to believe. Truth is, there are alien cows among us. You heard me right: robot cows from a distant galaxy where they doubtless raise, milk, fatten up and eat human beings. Perhaps you think me mad? Well, you wouldn't be the first. Or even the second. In fact, please take a number. Nevertheless, consider this...

Shortly after my wife and I moved into our new abode here in Bucolia, surrounded by my father-in-law Vernon's quietly grazing beef cattle, a most peculiar thing happened.

It took three months for the phone company to hook up a hard line from their very own poles only a hundred or so feet across the road from our front door. Now, that's not the peculiar thing. Anyone who's ever dealt with a utility company knows that the simplest tasks may require rivers of time and landfills of paperwork to complete. In our case, instead of connecting the lines from pole to pole to house, our phone company found it necessary to dig a trench and run our line under the road. Looking back, I'm amazed it took a mere three months. The end result: we had phone service and a spiffy green junction box buried in the cow pasture containing phone lines leading from said trench to aforementioned home.

A few weeks later, the customary autumn rains began to fall. And our phone service began to fail. A typical call would go something like this:

Ring! Ring. (Ring?)

Us: Hello?

Caller: Lo this Xlmtprs! How thgsathe yew hobo?

Us: Hello? Is this (insert random name here)? I can hardly hear you!

Caller: Cad herboyu eder. Lebbe cawback.

Us: Call back? Yes, please!

Subsequent returned calls would degenerate into shouting matches involving attempts at monosyllabic communication, Morse code, and, eventually, something resembling Sanskrit. The culprit, I ingeniously deducted, was most likely water in the phone lines.

But soon the ringing of the phone itself devolved into feeble squawks that finally ceased altogether. From my workplace, I called the phone company, which promised to swiftly dispatch a technician.

Weeks later, I received a call at work from said technician. He was laughing. Oddly, I was not amused. "You know," he chuckled, "I've been doing this job for 17 years and I've never seen anything like this. I've traced your problem to the junction box out in the pasture. The cap's been chewed off and all the phone wires have been dragged out. Found some of 'em 20 feet away. Looks like your cows ate 'em up like a bowl of spaghetti," he guffawed.

"Not *my* damn cows," I fumed.

"Huh?"

"They're not *my* cows. Father-in-law's. Can you fix it?" My mind's eye began to envision my next encounter with Vernon. Definitely a PG encounter: adult language, some graphic violence. Who knows, maybe an R rating might be in the offing.

"Oh sure. Just a simple re-wire. Put a more permanent cap on it. Golly, looks like they had quite the feast out here," howled the repairman.

"Heh-heh," I growled.

"Or maybe it's like one of those alien movies where the guy gets his guts tore out and they show his innards strewn all over kingdom come."

"Just give me a call when you're finished."

"Never seen anything like it!"

"Thank you."

"My pleasure. Wait'll I tell the boys back at the office. Hoo-eee!"

And so it was that the bovine minions had attempted to cut off our line of communication. A classic battle strategy that nearly worked. However, that was not the end of it.

For, later that year, I happily strung gloriously multicolored Halloween lights along the pasture fence line, joyously humming Halloween carols as I toiled. Such carols generally involve stewing corpses in pots as opposed to decking halls. Admittedly, Halloween carols haven't quite caught on yet. Give it time. Anyhow, plugged in, the lights glowed eerily, proudly displaying our Halloween spirit for all Bucolia to see. My heart leapt with ghoulish glee.

Then, a few days later, one string of lights failed. A day or two after that, more lights winked out. My gorgeously lit fence line was beginning to resemble a snaggle-toothed monster. Upon close inspection, I discovered a broken bulb here, a frayed wire there, a mangled plug…all dripping with some sort of disgusting slimy, sticky substance. Was this the nefarious work of ghosts or goblins? No. This was plain and simple a cud attack.

The damn cows had eaten my Halloween lights!

Now, call me paranoid (they all do, don't they?), but you tell me: What kind of cow feeds on electrical cords? Give up? Well, I'll tell you what kind of cow feeds on electrical cords…

Robot cows. Alien cows. Cows whose sole purpose is to battle, isolate, confuse, confound and otherwise harass human beings. Their ultimate goal: dominance over the human species, either by our capitulation to their terrorist tactics or…our complete eradication from the face of the earth, pasture by pasture.

I don't know where these cows come from, but I'm keeping an eye on them. Soon I'll uncover their tactics and chain of command. I may oppose enhanced interrogation and extraordinary rendition when it comes to us humans, but against these bovines? Anything goes.

Meanwhile, watch the fields, my friends. They're out there. They're plotting. They're pooping. They're mooing in code. And if your cable connection gets fuzzy or your Christmas lights go dim? Be afraid. Be very afraid.

Or, be proactive. Haul out your tongs, basters, and flippers; and fire up your grill!

Part IV: "Guys with Buns"

As you can see, dear readers, much like ill-advised incursions by self-righteous westerners into the Middle East, the Battle of the Hillside drags on. I lash corn stalks to the fence posts in celebration of fall harvest? The cows eat them. I tie political signs to the wire fence in celebration of my naïve devotion to the electoral process? Into one of several bovine stomachs they disappear. We invite guests over for a formal dinner? Guess who decides to hang around the fence line in plain view, peeing and pooping in great gushing streams of disgusting effluvia, leering menacingly at our friends who've suddenly lost their appetites. These terrorist tactics must be stopped. We've got to soldier on, eschewing any well-intentioned tendency toward vegetarianism.

Therefore, it is that I humbly submit the following battle anthem—to be sung to the tune of "Cows with Guns"—with massive apologies to imaginative songwriter and visionary activist Dana Lyons (www.cowswithguns.com).

Rise up, lads, don your silly aprons, arm yourselves with flammable fluid, matches, propane and mesquite, and let us lift our victorious voices as we gather our seasonings, marinades and condiments. All together now...

"GUYS WITH BUNS"

Hefty and hungry, looking for beef to munch
Cuz that's what's for dinner, breakfast and lunch
Guys with buns

Raised on steaks from well done to rare
Dreaming of Angus, the best of cow fare
Eat like Huns

They'll settle for Hereford, even burgers will do
But won't eat no veggies, 'less they come in beef stew
Arteries are numb

Sure, they'll load on the pickles with thick slabs of onion
But mustard and ketchup? Matters of opinion.
Piled high fun

They worship the Barbeque Bible, they burn the Qowran
Sesame, sourdough, whole wheat, that's in their holy plan
Buns with aplomb

A cow's greatest fear may not be cold weather
Or seeing a biker all clad in pure leather
A cow's greatest fear will be now and forever
Catching a glimpse of a fat guy with a beer and a Weber

Chorus: *All hail to Carnivore Kingdom*
And hoist your tongs on high
We will fight for the right to barbeque,
Broil, and even fry!
Guys with buns

Into the breach, laddies! Spare neither Angus nor Hereford. Give 'em all you got, from A-1 to Zatarain's, arteries be damned.

Matthew Thuney

Chapter 5: Herdology 101

Part I: A City Dweller's Guide to Cattle

Having somewhat successfully survived the legendary Battle of the Hillside, wherein I was outnumbered, surrounded and constantly menaced by mean-spirited bovine minions—and being hitched to a born-and-bred farm gal who most definitely knows her way around livestock—you might assume that by now I've acquired immense knowledge regarding the nature and behavior of cattle. You might assume that the University of Bucolia has seen fit to bestow upon me a Doctorate of Herdology; that I'm invited to speak at conferences discussing the devious ways of bovine behavior and their dastardly plot to overthrow humanity.

You might want to reassess those assumptions after hearing what I *think* I *might* know when it comes to cows. Namely the following not-so-learned observations...

I feel fairly certain that the scientific name for the common American cow-type creature is or ought to be Bovinus Diabolicus ("Cloven-hoofed Devil-spawn") or Effluviosis Maximus ("Perpetual Pooper"). How cattle can be considered sacred by any culture is a Mystery for the Ages, alongside "Who Built the Pyramids," "What the Hell is a Sphinx," and women. Just women. In general.

Cows come in two basic colors: black or brown. Variations are available for a slight surcharge. Such as spots, for example. Large white spots, which can turn any simple bovine into quite the fashion plate. Or a seemingly uncalled-for proliferation of hair. Some Scottish breeds can prove to be immensely hairy, which is perfectly understandable. Especially if you've drunk enough Glenfiddich.

On the topic of horns, only male cattle grow them. It's just common sense: males and horns go together like hot dogs and mustard. There's a joke somewhere in there involving buns, but I don't *relish* the thought of telling it. Now, some delusional dairymen (and women as well) insist that female Bovinae Nefariosa ("Wily Woman Cowbeasts") can also sport horns. Clearly, this is nonsense, probably an old wives' tale. What in the world would old wives (or Bovinae

42

Nefariosa Bluehairia) do with horns? Such a mutation would be an abomination to both pasture and plate!

These same delusional dairypersons might try to tell you that the term "cow" properly refers only to adult females of the species. Poopycock! Are we to chastise and correct every curious child who innocently points at a fat-bellied, four-legged, giant-headed beast grazing languidly and crapping luxuriantly in a farmer's field and excitedly exclaims, "Look, mommy, cow!" Nay, I say. A cow is a cow and by any other name still stinks to high heaven. Besides, we parents have more pressing reasons to reprimand our offspring. Such as when they refuse to eat anchovies on their pizza or insist upon watching *SpongeBob SquarePants*.

Likewise, befuddled farmers often adopt terms like "bull" or "steer" when referring to male cattle who may or may not remain equipped with their male...well...equipment. It's a simple matter of po-*tay*-to po-*tah*-to. Cows are cows: dastardly and destructive yet ultimately delicious.

As we've learned from previous encounters with the bovine kingdom, your typical cow consumes grass, hay, telephone wires, and Halloween lights. These foodstuffs are rapidly transformed into a foul-smelling gelatinous goo, which is almost instantaneously evacuated into massive reeking piles of poop to which human feet are mysteriously drawn via what physicists refer to as a "strange attractor." Hence the debilitating disability common among herdsmen known as "poopfoot." A similar strange attractor is thought to be at work in urban areas, wherein human feet and dog feces are unceremoniously united.

But just between you, me, and the fencepost (assuming said fencepost is not being wiretapped by the Bovine Security Agency or BSA), cows can be controlled. Two methods yield the best results.

First, if you find yourself cowed by one tyrannical bovine in particular, give that beast a name. Preferably a demeaning one. Many cultures teach that by naming a thing we gain control over it. Although this theory has not been shown to be effective with regard to human children. Nonetheless, my wife Donna employed this technique to great advantage with a herd of cattle who were ruled by a particularly large and menacing beast, possibly the offspring of the legendary terrorist Enrique. This bully would lead his pack hither and yon wantonly across our fields, stopping only to sneer at Donna and I through the pasture fence whenever he had a mind to. So Donna conjured a calming appellation for the fiendish brute, namely "Puddin' Cup." At first, Puddin' Cup merely scoffed at his new moniker, but when Donna began repeatedly calling him by name in a cloying, cutesy-poo voice, Puddin' Cup's fellow gang members started to snicker and chuckle at their beleaguered leader. One day, we noticed that Puddin' Cup had relinquished his top cow status to a somewhat smaller, leaner, quicker member of the pack. Gradually, he fell further and further back down the line to the status of straggler, trailing behind a rather goofy specimen of a cow with a loopy grin and lazy eye. Puddin' Cup's days of sneer and swagger were over, and peace ruled the pasture.

If humiliation isn't your preferred modus operandi, you might want to go with intimidation. I suggest a proven tactic called "Givin' 'em the Stink Eye." First, select the animal you wish to dominate. Then, make absolutely certain there's an impenetrable barrier between you and said animal. Lure your target toward you with irresistible bait: some fresh grass, tasty hay, or nice length of extension cord. As the cow-beast approaches within reach, lay the Stink Eye on 'im! That is, squinch your eye up into an evil squint, twist your mouth into a grotesque leer, think medium-rare thoughts, and look that son-of-a-heifer straight in the eye.

The result? Soon enough the menacing bull, steer, cow, or future rump roast will eventually turn away and lumber off to a far side of the pasture. You will have taught that potential miscreant a valuable lesson. Namely that you're quite clearly a completely crazed cow-hating bigot. A completely crazed cow-hating bigot who had better watch his back next time he wanders beyond the safety of a fence into the arena of the pasture. Once a cowrilla terrorist has honed into your backside and built up a good head of steam, even the Stink Eye cannot save your hide.

Next, we'll consult our textbook, *To Serve Cattle*, and learn how we humans can best accommodate our bovine friends.

Part II: To Serve Cattle

Settle down, class. Susie, kindly remove that chewing gum from your mouth...unless you brought enough to share with everyone? I thought not. Tommy, put your cell phone away unless you'd like to see it have a most unfortunate close encounter with the back wall of the classroom. Thank you. Now to the task at hand, namely our continuation of the fascinating study of cows I like to call "Herdology 101."

To Serve Cattle, the ancient go-to text regarding the proper relationship between human and bovine, is thought to have been written by Stuartius of Andersonium, a Greek philosopher of the Epicurean School and founder of the legendary secret society, Black Knights of the Angus. While the original manuscript of *To Serve Cattle* has been quite literarily marinated and tenderized nearly beyond recognition through the ages, the guiding principal of this iconic work remains clear:

Human beings can best serve cattle...on a platter. Preferably with fresh asparagus and garlic mashed potatoes.

Now, some moon-eyed cow pie loving fancypants leather-haters have objected to this line of thought over the years. But the gods have seen fit to arrange it so that carnivores reproduce more rapidly than vegetarians do, so that the natural order of man over cow is properly maintained and the world is made safe from cowpression and cowtatership. This is the ultimate genius of the message of *To Serve Cattle*, although the text does fail to solve certain riddles.

Mostly, these mysteries are a matter of taste, a delicious dichotomy as it were: Angus or Hereford? To sauce or not to sauce? Ah yes, my friends, questions for the ages.

In our previous session, we delved into the madness of herdsmen. How, for instance, they insist upon separating cattle into fairy-tale classes like bull, steer, heifer. And when it comes to the finished product—dare I say meat—cattle farmers are equally daft. They cannot agree on such a simple question as, which better suits the palate, Angus or Hereford? Some crazed cattlemen brazenly claim there is no difference whatsoever. Others have been known to argue for days, shouting at each other and gesticulating wildly over their respective fences. "Hail Hereford!" "Angus is king!" The warring can continue for days until a tractor jousting match breaks out, one farmer mounting his John Deere, the other astride his Massey Ferguson, sharpened fence posts at the ready.

But close exegesis of *To Serve Cattle* in the original Greek reveals Stuartius of Andersonium's true views on the topic. Hereford is meant for those who simply don't like the taste of beef; Angus is for those who do. To wit…

An insipid, inferior brand of meat, Hereford beef is lean and blasé. It's best when cooked at low temperature for a long period of time, preferably in gravy or water. The result? A tender yet taste-free wasteland of culinary nothingness bereft of natural juices. Pour on the sauces grandma; because that's the only flavor you'll get out of this perfunctory patty.

On the other hand—or the other hoof—Angus properly prepared is a wonderland of taste and texture. And by properly prepared I mean just barely cooked. A marbelous (that's right, I said marbelous on account of the Angus breed's propensity toward thick lines of luscious fat)…as I say, a marbelous playground of juice and meat, Angus virtually begs to be eaten raw. But certain sissypants health officials require meat to be heated to a minimum temperature, so rather than spending time in nutritionally correct prison (or perhaps the emergency ward), we good citizen carnivores must bow to their petty demands.

A final addendum regarding that elusively mysterious volume known as "The Abomination of Sauces," a semi-apocryphal text which may or may not have been part of Stuartius of Andersonium's original thesis. The fundamental culinary question is simply this: should a perfectly good steak be subjected to the slathering on of artificial additives in the form of marinades or other gooey concoctions? The answer may not be found in *To Serve Cattle*, but even a cursory reading of the adjunct text *First Texans* (chapter eleven, verse thirteen) reveals this: "Neither shalt thou take up thy brush nor thy tube nor thy neighbor's bottle for the desecration of thy T-Bone for the sinful intent of basting."

Amen, and so mote it be. Praise the Lord and pass the mashed potatoes!

That's all for today, class. There'll be a quiz on Friday, so don't forget your Blue Books, Merlot and J.A. Henckels cutlery.

Matthew Thuney

Chapter 6: The Witching Well

Part I: How Do You Know She's a Witch?

When you think of the word bucolic, what images come to mind?

Maybe you envision flowing fields of swaying grain or fresh green grass; inviting woods teaming with maple, ash, cedar; birds flitting about, chirping away in merry concert; rolling rivers, trickling streams; flowers smiling in the sun; cottages, churches, chapels, country stores; tractors, pickups, plows; cows, horses, sheep, goats; farmers chatting over their fences, neighbors sharing casseroles and pies, kids riding their bikes up and down shady lanes. Yes, we have all that here in Bucolia. You'll probably find it somewhere in the contract for living here. Just click on "Terms of Agreement."

But witches and wolves, Bigfeet and bears, cougars and specters? Not likely part of your mental picture. Not included in the glossy, tri-fold, full color "Welcome to Bucolia" brochure. Rarely discussed in churches or chapels or over farm fences.

You might not expect the unexpected when you cross over our river and through our woods, but it's out there. Oh yes, it's out there.

Before our home even attempted to come over the mountain, I was introduced to the eerie side of Bucolia. Prior to planting any sort of domicile out here in the hinterlands, you need to secure a source of water. Apparently, it's necessary for preparing meals, washing clothes, growing crops, making ice cubes, filling up the kids' plastic swimming pool so the adults can splash around in it, living. Little things like that.

Water, at least in this neck of the woods, calls for a well.

And that's where the witch came in.

Being from the city, where all things are allegedly done by the book (said book being located somewhere in the depths of City Hall, guarded by a cadre of hand-picked bureaucrats), I naively assumed that in order to site and dig a well one would enlist the assistance of a professional well digger. Perhaps some high-falutin' engineer with lots of degrees after his name who would be affiliated with a well-drilling conglomerate headquartered in Dallas, New York City or at least Seattle.

But that's not the way things are done in Bucolia. No, if there's a Book of Bucolia it's probably hidden away in a deep, dark cave or abandoned cloister, guarded by a glowering dragon and an elite troupe of steely-eyed elves. If you want something done in Bucolia, you have to "ask around." Presumably, by "asking around" you'll find someone who has read the Book.

So that's just what we did. We asked around and got the phone number of a local witch. A water witch, to be precise.

Now, yours truly is no stranger to strange things. For instance, I've had a lifelong fascination with UFOs. Those doggone lights in the sky, craft on the ground, and all the weird humanoid critters seen walking around and visiting folks at inconvenient times must mean something. They don't all emanate from swamply vapors, tricksy reflections or the overheated imaginations of slightly skewed minds. When pilots and policemen, soldiers and seamen, regularly report such encounters—folks who generally know what they're looking at—then you have to sit up and take notice. And that happens all the friggin' time.

Yet when my wife Donna recommended that we consult a water witch, all my acceptance of unexplained phenomena was put rudely on hold. After all, we were talking about our future water supply here. No place for airy-fairy tomfoolery, right?

So I asked around some more. Sure enough, seems like almost everyone in Bucolia had the help of a water witch in siting their wells.

We decided to go with a gal who descended from a long line of diviners.

Called her up, and she met us at our property one strange, fine day.

The witch brought with her a mysterious array of divining devices, but the one she personally used looked like something out of Star Trek. Or more likely Lord of the Rings. Sitting atop a metal handle was a crystal enclosure into which she would insert a sample of whatever she was looking for. Which wasn't always water. Might be a bit of fur if it were a lost pet or article of clothing for a lost person. She came highly recommended, and proceeded to validate that praise.

Donna's dad Vernon, who had lived on the land for eons and had his own well successfully dowsed, joined us in our sloping hillside field as we all selected various rods (none as fancy as the witch's, mind you). I held two wire rods, one in each hand, and Donna grasped a similar contraption. When the rods crossed in front of you, there be the water. I think Vernon used a coat hanger. That's all he needed. No high-tech silliness for that wizened veteran.

We set off up the slope, me staggering and stumbling along over the rocky, uneven ground in my city shoes, while the others moseyed along at a steady pace.

Nothing much happened with my dowsing rods, so I amused myself just twisting and turning them this way and that. Apparently, I don't have "the gift" for dowsing. Or walking, for that matter. But Donna soon had a hit.

"I think I've got something," Donna said excitedly. "Show-off," I thought. Sure enough, Donna's dowsers were definitely crossed. We all trudged over to her spot.

"Oh yes, it's water all right," said the water witch. I began to seethe with envy. "But it's not potable. You don't want to be drinking this water," she advised. "I could've told you that," I thought smugly.

"How can you tell?" asked Donna.

The water witch pointed to her own magical Gandalf gun, "I put clean drinking water in here, and it's not reacting to the water you just found." And with that, she turned around and headed back up the hill.

"Oh," said Donna and I. Vernon just grunted, as if we should have known better.

While the water witch ventured ever upward, I wondered aloud why the swale at the lowest corner of our property wouldn't be the perfect place for a well. Donna looked at me as though I were a small child, slowly saying, "Because that's where all the runoff gathers, with all the potential impurities like pesticides from neighboring fields, our own precious cow poop and such. If anyplace out here is going to be polluted, it's right there."

"Oh," I said. Vernon shook his head and grunted. Twice.

Near the very top of the hill, close to where pasture gave way to woods, the water witch halted.

"Here," she said simply, "Right here. Nice, clean water between 50 to 55 feet down." I wasn't about to ask how she could be that precise. Enough humiliation for me for one day. Even Vernon looked a bit skeptical, but he duly pounded a stake into the very spot.

We thanked the water witch, and offered to pay her a tidy sum for her services. "No thank you," she said. "Pay it forward. Next time someone needs your help, do it for free." That's the way things get done in Bucolia: ask around, pay it forward. Though I couldn't imagine then someone actually needing help from me. But that time would come.

Next step: find a reputable well digger. We asked around…

Part II: Can You Dig it? For Ten Grand, Sure!

As it turns out, well diggers—even here in the hinterlands—don't come cheap. Apparently, it takes more than some picks and shovels and a handful of guys in hardhats and suspenders with strong backs. There's massive equipment involved and a bunch of sciencey stuff dealing with geology, testing and all manner of puzzling paperwork. In fact, not many companies are qualified to perform such work, and (you guessed it) they charge an arm, a leg, and, if your terra is a tad too firma and puts up uninvited resistance, possibly an ear.

All of which I wish I'd given thought to before placing our expensive fate in the hands of the water witch. What if she was wrong? I might just lose both ears in the process. Nonetheless, we put our faith in the Water Gods, crossed our fingers like fleshly divining rods, and hoped for the best.

Besides, Donna attempted (mostly in vain, I freely admit) to allay my apprehension with the story of Vernon's well-digging experience. Vernon had hired a reputable firm to locate and bore a shaft for his water supply, and the results were less than spectacular. The diggers ran into a dry spot, shrugged resignedly, packed up their equipment and scurried away, leaving poor Vern with nothing but lots of rock, sand, and a hefty invoice for services rendered. Whereupon he asked around to find another set of diggers and a water witch to guide them. That old well has been pumping out oodles of sweet water for Donna's dad ever since.

The ask-around network put us in touch with a reputable well-drilling outfit that had probably been in existence since Joseph got into deep trouble with his Coat of Many Colors.

Ten thousand dollars later — for that, we could have supplied Joseph with quite the jazzy wardrobe—the drilling team arrived on our property and promptly headed for the very same swale at the lowest corner of the property I had suggested for the site. Fortunately for us, being blissfully ignorant in town at our day jobs, Vernon wandered over and confronted the wayward diggers.

"Not down here," growled Vernon, "up there!" And he motioned wildly up the hill to where the water witch's siting stake stuck out of the hillside. The drillers looked at Vernon as though he were several cups short of a full bucket, but dutifully followed him up the slope.

There they set up their immense equipment and commenced burrowing. Ten, twenty, thirty, forty feet they drilled down. Lots of sand, rock and clay. No water. When they reached fifty feet, they stopped. "There's no sign of an aquifer here, sir," they informed Vernon.

Vernon, who had no earthly idea what an aquifer might be and probably couldn't hear them anyway since, as usual, he'd forgotten his hearing aid, simply pointed at the ground and shouted, "Keep diggin'! Water witch said 50 to 55 feet!"

By now, somewhat bemused by the whole scene, and secure in the knowledge that they had our ten grand in the bank already and would gleefully charge us more for re-siting the well, the drilling team was more than happy to fire up their monstrosity again. So they kept on a-diggin'.

And there it was: at precisely 54 feet, a free-flowing river of underground water just waiting to dance its way into our new home's waiting pipes. Still, there was one more hurdle to jump. A chemist had to test the H2O to make sure it was fit for human consumption.

Turns out it was fit as a weight lifter: pure and clean, but a bit high in iron. Good old country hardwater. Keep you plowing through life for years to come.

Out here in Bucolia, between the old ways and modern technology, we sit pretty comfortably in the here and now.

Chapter 7: Magical Bucolia

Part I: Our Friend Anna

Some of us, whether or not we live in magical places, are fortunate enough to have magical friends. Folks who just seem to be in tune with greater forces, who just seem to be aware of things that you or I or just about anybody else would not have access to. For the most part, we probably think of these friends as a bit kooky or somewhat odd. They don't just wander off the beaten path; they seem to have camped out there, permanently. Whether that existential campsite finds them holed up in a small apartment in the midst of a bustling city or a ramshackle hovel perched in a peat bog, these wonderfully curious folk seem to be content to live on a different plane, and our own wonderful curiosity seems to keep drawing us to them.

So it was, and is, with our dear friend Anna. She barged into our lives one day and hasn't left since. Occasionally exasperating, always interesting, forever giving with open arms and heart, Anna kept Donna and I on our toes, spiritually speaking, and proved to be the source of many an inspired thought or moment.

Anna gifted us with several of those moments even before our house had arrived on our property.

We had asked Anna to come out to Bucolia and bless our land. To ward off evil occurrences and invite good energy. It just seemed like an Anna thing to do, and she was happy to do it for us. This involved visiting the four corners of the property, placing special crystals there, and saying words of safekeeping, welcome, and spiritual cleansing.

As Anna, Donna, and I traversed the fields, a few strange events took place. Well, strange by our standards, but quite mundane by Anna's.

After placing the first crystal, Anna started discussing the Sasquatch who frequented our woods in the same manner that you or I might talk about a visit from an old friend. In a very matter-of-fact tone, Anna relayed to us that the Sasquatch People were very pleased that we had decided not to place our house farther up on the hillside (as we had originally planned), because that spot in the woods was one which they and their friends the deer frequented from time to time. That particular place was where the deer liked to rest during their daily routine, and where the Sasquatch also liked to pause and take in the beauty of our valley as they passed from one locale to another. Oddly, Donna and I had decided a few months earlier that, although that location would have offered a breathtaking view of the valley and surrounding hills and mountains, it just didn't feel right. As though we would be intruding, somehow.

After placing the second crystal, Anna paused as we walked our western fence line. "Something happened here," she frowned. "An animal passed away on this spot. A calf? Very sad." I had no idea what she might be talking about, but the look on Donna's face was one of astonished recognition and remembrance. After all, Donna had been raised on this land, had helped her father and brothers tend to the cattle who roamed there. True enough, she recalled a childhood incident in which she had come upon a dying calf on that very spot. It was an emotional moment in her life, and apparently one that had left its spiritual mark in the real world.

That's funny: I say real world as though we human beings know what is real. In all honesty, I do not believe we can lay claim to such certainty. We like to think we're the masters of reality, the gatekeepers of knowledge and truth. But every time we're certain that we've finally constructed an all-encompassing version of reality, a wave of mystery wells up unexpectedly from the impenetrably vast ocean of the universe and washes that sand castle away.

So it was in the presence of Anna that day. Mystery upon mystery seemed to inhabit and enliven the land. Finally, it came time to find the center of our property so that Anna might invoke one last, all-encompassing blessing. As we trudged around the field, attempting to discern a likely, spiritually special nexus, we noticed a hawk flying, circling just above. Now, there's nothing extremely remarkable about a hawk in the sky over Bucolia. They visit us quite often. Our fields are a buffet of rodentia for raptors. Nonetheless, the spectacle of a hawk soaring overhead is quite breathtaking.

When at last we could shift our gaze from sky to ground and resume our search for the heart of the property, we were astonished to find a hawk feather lying not twenty feet from where we stood. Anna laughed her brilliant laugh, looked up at the hawk, raised her hands and shouted, "Thank you!" Sometimes you hear people talk about receiving signs when they're trying to figure something out, trying to reach an important decision. To you, those signs might seem a bit vague, a rather tenuous coincidence, perhaps, on which to base such an important choice. But this sign? It might as well have been a garish, multicolored neon arrow pointing down from the sky directly to the very spot, declaring with blinding brilliance, "CENTER OF PROPERTY HERE!"

That was Anna. She was, as they say, "in tune" with Mother Nature. And she genuinely enjoyed walking around the outside of our home once it was in place, taking in the new plants Donna had brought to her gardens and relishing the fresh life blossoming forth. Anna especially seemed to take a shine to the fern garden on the north side of our home. But the path there was primitive, steep, and bumpy. Her aging hips and knees didn't cotton to that terrain. So Donna and I dug a long series of stepping-stones into the winding descent, to render the pathway more navigable for our dear friend. "Anna's Walk," we call it.

Anna passed from this plane to the next shortly after we completed that project. But we know she still walks there, pausing to gaze at the ferns and marvel at the red rhododendron that splashes its gaudy color all over the place when it blooms.

Whenever I was blessed enough to make Anna laugh—which I tried to do whenever possible, because she seemed to need and appreciate humor more than most—she would break out with the most musical, melodious burst of mirth you ever wanted to hear (and you wanted to hear it a lot), followed by a hearty, "Thank you!" Just as she had with that mystical hawk.

But it was always Anna we should have been thanking. And we still do.

Part II: Faery Lights

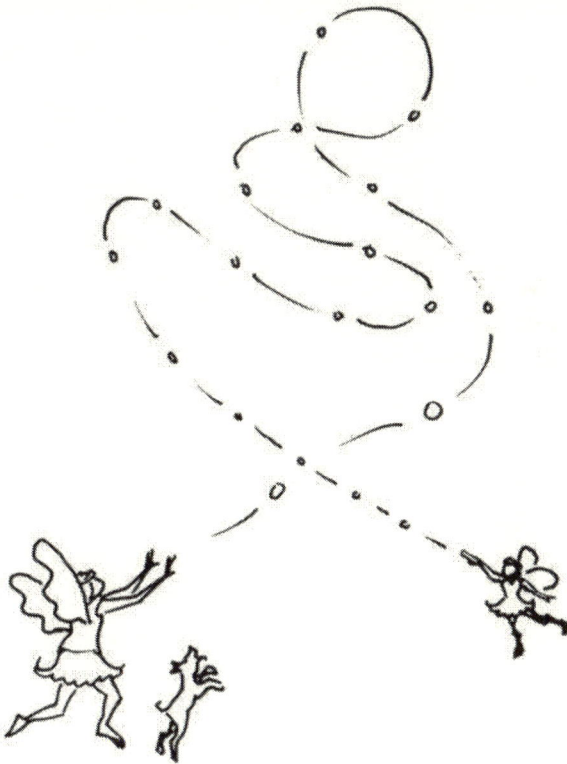

Some aspects of Bucolia are magical in more subtle ways. Take, for example, the Night of the Faery Lights.

What are faery lights? Difficult to say, exactly. The legend and the sightings have been passed down throughout human history. A ring of lights dancing in a field, a bright orb or two flitting from tree to tree in a forest, a luminescent glow in a gifted garden. Mystical beacons that have historically been associated with the "wee folk," tiny creatures who assist Mother Nature with Her work of keeping our world vibrant with life and awe.

And so it was a brilliantly clear spring night in Bucolia, which found Donna and I, our daughter Rachel and granddaughter Miranda sitting on our front deck, gazing up at the riot of stars splashed across the sky. UFOs have long been a fascination of mine, and I had ensnared the rest of the family in the search for mysterious nighttime lights as well. Fortunately, this was a particularly active night for shooting stars, if not for zigzagging or hovering oddities.

Little Miranda was utterly enraptured by shooting stars, exclaiming with great glee every time she spotted one streaking across the sky. It soon became a contest between her and me to see who could spy the most shooting stars, not to mention who could shout, "Oooooh!!" the loudest. Donna, Rachel, and any neighbors within earshot, no doubt thought us quite mad. One of those glorious occasions when family really is family and there's nothing but fun, wonder, and laughter to be had. But as the light show died down and Miranda's eyelids began to droop, it was evident that our junior astronomer's bedtime had come.

With Miranda tucked in, the three alleged adults returned to the observation post in front of the house for one last peek at what the night had to offer. We were not disappointed.

Our eyes were suddenly distracted from the sky above to our neighbor's field to the north. Something strange, something quite bright, was bobbing along the horizon there. Naturally, my initial instinct (perhaps fueled by several glasses of Merlot), was to shout, "UFO!" But that seemed unlikely, even to me, since the mystery light in question appeared to be somewhat small as it traversed the field. Perhaps trace energy from a landed spacecraft? A light emanating from the wandering occupant of said craft? No, something else. I searched my memory for applicable samples from myth and folklore. Then it came to me. That's it! Faery lights!

I rapidly attempted to explain the background of this phenomenon to Donna and Rachel, as we made our way from the front of the house to the back, where the light was more readily visible. But, addled by wine and befuddled by excitement, my mumbled explanation served only to confuse and mystify the situation even more. "Nature! Wee folk! Celtic! Sprites! Druids! Stonehenge!" I exclaimed.

Sure enough, there was that bewildering light, seemingly flying, gliding, bouncing, rolling across the adjoining field, bright and amazing as the streaking lights we had witnessed earlier up in the sky. It was a hypnotic vision, and we all looked on trying to discern its meaning as the spectacle continued.

Finally, I decided I had to take a closer look. Donna dashed into the house, grabbed the two pairs of binoculars, kept one, and gave one to me. As I made my way closer to the neighbor's property, binoculars jiggling crazily in front of my unfocused eyes while I staggered over the cow-trodden mounds and gullies, Donna gave me a blow-by-blow description of the ongoing sighting from the well-grounded security of our back yard.

"Strange," she called out to me, "The light seems to glide from right to left, but sometimes stops in the middle, twirls around, and sort of bounces back one way or the other!"

At long last, my creaky knees and reluctant ankles having objected mightily to this jagged nighttime jaunt, I judged myself close enough to stand still and examine this bizarre spectacle from a relatively close distance. Raising the binoculars to my weary eyes, I made an amazing discovery. "Wait!" I shouted over my shoulder to Donna and Rachel, who were hanging on my every word. "There *is* something interfering with the passage of the light!" I refocused the ocular goggles for maximum perusal. My heart sank. "Aw crap," I relayed to the expectant duo.

There was indeed a creature intercepting the light as it flew from one point to the other. A four-legged creature. With a tail.

"It's a dog," I sighed loudly, watching as the decidedly earthly beast leapt up to grab the light between its jaws. Then the dog jogged and hopped happily from midpoint to the intended goal of the flickering flyer. "And our neighbors," I related sadly to Donna and Rachel, having recognized the two objects between which the previously magical light traversed.

Our neighbors had chosen that night to play a harmless game of catch with their dog and, of course, a lighted Frisbee. So much for faery lights in Bucolia.

But there was one magical creature who had blessed us with her presence that night. She was sound asleep and dreaming of shooting stars in our guest bedroom. And the very next year, another miracle came into our lives in the form of our second grand-daughter Alison, gifted to us by our son David and daughter-in-law Dey. Nowadays Miranda and Alison delight in playing together. Soon enough, it will be time for us to buy them a Frisbee. With lights.

Part III: Drumming up a Wolf

So we've established a few things about Bucolia. Strange things, abby-normal things, it's true. Like there be witches in Bucolia, that's for sure. Bigfoot in Bucolia? So the legends say, and so the evidence might indicate. But can a supposedly rare creature be conjured up simply by pounding on a drum?

Here in Bucolia, the answer is, "Of course; you need to ask?"

It was a crisp, clear autumn evening—one of the first crisp, clear autumn evenings for my wife Donna and I to enjoy shortly after our home was dragged over the mountain and through the woods. The kind of autumn evening that brings to mind crunchy apples, plump pumpkins, the glorious golden array of leaves swaying and shimmering in the freshly conjured fall breeze. You could fill your lungs with that breeze and your heart with those sights and, live in that moment with peace, joy, and dreams of delicious pie forever.

But me? I was hauling our garbage and recycling bins down to the roadside. My lungs were trying to repel the stink of decay and my heart was questioning why in the hell we'd decided on such a long driveway in the first place.

Inside the house, Donna wasn't faring much better. She'd suffered through a rather stressful day at work, and her back was registering severe complaints about the extent of gardening she'd done the previous weekend. So I'd left Donna to her relaxations and ruminations while I performed my husbandly duty.

Things went from bad to worse—more precisely from dull drudgery to astonished anger—when, as I wheeled our trashcan streetside, I felt a slight tug on my lower arm.

Now, you might recall that Donna's dad Vernon was running cattle around our hillside home at this time. And with cattle comes fencing. And with cattle fencing comes that amazing invention known as barbed wire. Or "Bob Wire," as Vernon called it. Possibly Vernon (being of Polish descent) is of the opinion that some clever fella named Robert Wirinski came up with the idea. Be that as it may…

I thought nothing of this slight tug on my arm until I had all the disposables and recyclables neatly in place for pickup and began trudging back up the hellishly long driveway. At which point I absentmindedly swiped at the spot of the slight tug with my opposite hand. That hand, oddly enough, came away covered in something red.

Gazing down at my right arm, I quickly found the source of this mysterious red substance: there lay a bright red swath of blood about an inch and a half long. Title this lesson, "Matt moves to Bucolia and learns first-hand about the efficacy of barbed wire."

I was stunned and stopped in my tracks. But that particular stunning didn't last long, for, as I reached in my back pocket for my handy handkerchief (yes, life-long allergies do keep me prepared for nose-blowing and first aid) and began dabbing at the thin red line, I began hearing the most peculiar thing. Re-stunned, I held the handkerchief firmly against my arm and listened.

Rhythm, they say, possesses all manner of unique properties. Rhythm can make even the most clod-footed klutz want to dance. I can personally attest to that. Rhythm can make you feel good. Many native cultures claim that rhythm has healing powers. But that evening, rhythm made this bedraggled, bloodied former urbanite believe in the magic of Bucolia. Again.

So there I stood, stock-still, halfway up my driveway, bleeding profusely, yet listening raptly to the sound of what I could only imagine might be the beat of a drum. Was a long-lost tribe of indigenous warriors ensconced in our woods, communicating plans for an all-out assault upon our intrusive dwelling? Had Vernon's cattle simply straggled up unto trees, spied my approach, and decided to warn one another by pounding, hoof on bark, "Oh boy, here comes that new guy who can't tell a bull from a heifer. Get a load of him: cut his arm on the barbed wire! Let's see if he can make it back home before he bleeds out. Tee-hee, tee-hee." Or perhaps some innocent nature-loving interlopers had stumbled upon our woods and found them a suitable place for communing with earth, rock, and tree.

But as I cautiously approached our new abode, it began to dawn on me that the drumming was emanating not from hillside woods, but from the very house itself. Sure enough, with my good arm I opened the back door to find Donna pounding away on a native American drum I had bought her as a recovery gift following thyroid surgery a couple of years back. She often found solace in the rhythmic practice of drumming; solace from worldly woes and a sense of reconnection to the things that really mattered in life. From time to time, in fact, Donna and I have been known to get together with our friends and neighbors, sit around a fire pit, and drum like a band of crazy pagans. Which, come to think of it, we probably are! You really oughta try it sometime; I highly recommend it. Good for what ails ya, you'll likely laugh like mad and talk of things you'd never dreamed you would.

So when I saw Donna drumming inside the house and all by herself, I knew she'd had a really terribly awful no-good day. But I can top that, I thought, I damn near cut my arm off!

"Hey there, Hiawatha," I said, with my usual unsurpassed talent for spoiling a moment, "What's up?"

"Oh, my back's been killing me all day, and I had to sit through a bunch of meetings at work. Doesn't feel like I got anything done, and my back hurts worse than ever," said Donna, clearly exhausted.

"Gee," I said, "That's too bad. Hey, wanna see what I just did to my arm? You won't believe it. I may need stitches!" But as I carefully peeled the handkerchief from my arm expecting great gouts of gore, there only appeared a slight band of red, already drying up and looking perfectly innocuous.

"Poor baby," intoned Donna, with a look that said, why on Earth couldn't I have married a less clumsy man, one not prone to such whining and complaining?

"Well it really hurts like hell," I began, adopting my customary posture of self-defense, when suddenly Donna cut me off.

She was staring out our living room window up the hillside toward the line where pasture meets woods. "Is that a coyote?" she asked, pointing to a particular spot where I could only see a bit of a darkish blob. Donna's visual acuity, it must be said, rivals that of an eagle. Mine would more closely approximate that of a bat. A bungling bat at that.

"Wait, that's no coyote," said Donna, "Too big. Too tall. What *is* that?"

In a rare feat of clear-headedness, I snatched up a nearby pair of binoculars and trained them on the blob. Adjusting the focus, I honestly could not believe my eyes. Staring right back at me, not 50 yards away, was a face I'd not seen in over 30 years. You see, back in the best-forgotten bachelor days of my mid-twenties, somehow I'd gotten hold of a wildlife poster that I plastered on the inside of my front door. Having seen it every day for several months, that image remained etched and catalogued in some catacomb of my mind. And that image was looking back at me right now. It was the image of a grey wolf.

Donna didn't need binoculars. She stood by the window with me and said, "It almost looks like a wolf!"

"It *is* a wolf," I said, transfixed. The wolf turned his gaze from me toward the cattle grazing in the field. He looked like he might be reading a menu, the kind with the pictures like you see at Denny's. Fumbling desperately with the binoculars, I finally disentangled the attached cord from around my neck, knocking my glasses askew in the process, and handed the long-range peepers feebly to Donna.

Too late. The wolf had turned his back and was trotting back into the woods. Nonetheless, Donna had caught a glimpse of its splendid coat and tail, had witnessed its easy gait as it loped away. "Yep, that's a wolf all right," she sighed.

Perhaps this particular wolf had been simply window-shopping, wasn't all that hungry, or preferred Angus to Hereford. Who knows?

What I do know is that creature could best be described as regal or majestic. Not adjectives you'd associate with your typical coyote or stray dog.

What I do know is that both Donna and I had been overcome with a sense of awe, a feeling of being blessed to see such a magnificent sight. You just don't see wolves much anymore, at least not in this corner of Bucolia. It's a real privilege when you do. I do know that Donna's drumming had something to do with that wolf appearing at that place and time.

And I do know that Donna and I forgot all about the disappointments, aches, and pains of the day. We began talking about how much we loved our new home, and shared our hopes and dreams instead.

Chapter 8: Birds of a Feather

One nice thing about living in Bucolia is you really get to know your neighbors. Well, generally speaking, that's a nice thing; I suppose there are exceptions. For instance, that know-it-all farmer down the road who insists on poking his nose into everybody's business and imparting his unsolicited wisdom. But he's the exception. And I digress.

Not long after our gigantic modular home had made its way over the mountain and been summarily deposited upon our property, folks from up and down the road stopped by to say hello, introduce themselves, and welcome us to the hinterlands. It was a refreshing change from living in the urbs and suburbs where you rarely get to know the people who live beside, across from, or, in some cases on top of or below you. Even the nosey sage down the road proved to be an occasional source of assistance and more than occasional source of amusement. I reckon that's an improvement over blasé anonymity.

So it was that our new neighbors across the road invited us to avail ourselves of their path down to the river, which brought an abrupt and watery end to their property. Likewise, we encouraged them to tromp through our woods up on the hillside and check out the seasonal waterfall and creek. I think Donna and I got the better end of that deal. We much prefer the comfort of a lawn chair beside a gently flowing river to the rocky slopes and turned ankles of a steep and windy grade.

And, so it was that one gorgeous summer afternoon Donna and I stood by the river's edge, taking in the placid breeze and soft sunshine, when we found ourselves in a scene snatched straight out of *Jurassic Park*. A bird was headed our way, and a big bird at that. As it swung gracefully around a bend in the river, it seemed to grow bigger and bigger. Huge wings swung slowly up and down as it glided just above the river's course, not 30 feet from us. It was a crane, but might just as well have been a pterodactyl for all we knew as Donna and I stood slackjawed, glued to the spot, our heads turning like crazy magnets as we watched the creature's progress. Gradually, the crane made its way around the next bend, disappearing as majestically and magically as it had come.

We looked at each other, grinning like kids. "Did you see that? It was amazing! Quick, let's grab the camera in case it comes ba..." Too late. For here, in identical graceful style and with equal majesty and magic, came another great crane, presumably its predecessor's mate. Again, Donna and I stood and watched like a couple of perfect fools, heads swiveling to follow the huge bird's progress.

Another archetypal Bucolic moment, just as with the gray wolf. I wish the same could be said of my encounters with cows, but that's a relationship that seemed doomed from the start.

Nonetheless, Donna and I have cultivated a curious kinship with our fine feathered friends here in Bucolia. Watching them come and go with the seasons, flitting about field and forest, river and garden, has become one of our favorite pastimes. We have the books and binoculars to prove it.

We like to challenge each other on the subject of bird identification. One of us will spot a winged interloper, pass the binoculars to the other for observation, then we'll both fly to one of several books on the topic of avian identification to try and discern which critter it be. Invariably, Donna will emerge victorious. With her eagle sight and penchant for noticing detail, she will gradually chip away at my excited attempts at absolutely certain recognition.

"What a fine example of a Chestnut-backed Chickadee that was," I'll muse confidently.

"Too big for a Chickadee," Donna will counter.

"Well, look at how the fellow was savaging our feeder," I'll argue, "Clearly he'd be a candidate for Weight Watchers."

"And the tail was a bit longer than you'd expect," Donna will observe.

"Maybe he just went to the bird salon, got an extension or something…"

"The wings were spotty, not striped."

"Avian measles might account for that…"

"And the eyes were red."

"Poor little fellow had a rough night following his salon treatment…"

"I think that might just have been a Spotted Towhee rather than a Chickadee, don't you?"

"Well, there's always the off chance that I might have missed a detail or two. Say, wasn't that a Variegated Titmouse that just flew by?"

There being no such thing as a Variegated Titmouse here in Bucolia or anywhere else known to humankind, I will have once again been gently reminded that Donna's powers of observation and (even more horrifying) of logical deduction are far superior to mine. It's humbling, true, but an act of discovery just the same. The next day, I can brag to acquaintances that I espied and identified a Spotted Towhee in our front yard! As long as Donna's not around to witness said boast. And assuming I can find anyone who might be in the least bit interested.

So we love to lure birds to our abode. Accordingly, we've scattered various and sundry feeders, baths, and suet containers throughout our front and back yards. Watching our amazing avian amigos flutter about and interact has proved to be a constant source of instruction and amusement. And not only to us humans. Since Karma and Neo, our adopted indoor kitties, displayed such interest in our fine feathered friends, I felt it only fitting to install a feeding tray right outside our bedroom window. The sight of little birdies pecking away only inches from their twitching noses and swishing tails provides Karma and Neo endless entertainment. It's like Cat Channel HDTV. Or, as Donna so aptly puts it, feline WonkaVision. Unfortunately, when the weather is nice and the windows are up, our screens do take quite a beating.

Little dudes like the aforementioned Chickadees and Towhees, along with their Finch and Junco pals, always seem to be flying around in their various seasons, adding color and life to the bucolic scenery.

Sadly, like most communities whether animal or human, there be bullies in them there trees. Our particular brand of bucolic bully is the lovely but socially challenged Blue Jay. Oh wait, make that *Steller's* Jay. I've made the unconscionable mistake of using imprecise terminology on many occasions, only to be swiftly and condescendingly corrected by everyone from know-it-all birders to wizened lumberjacks to precocious preschoolers.

The pretty yet pugnacious Steller's Jay is apparently the provincial bird of British Columbia, a legendary land of haze and mountain somewhere to the north of us. And, if you ask any of the finches hereabouts in Bucolia, British Columbia is right where those jays can stay.

These blue-crested bullies take pride in swooping down upon our crowded garden feeders, chasing all the little winged folk unceremoniously away, and spending the next few carefree moments hogging all the seeds, suet, nuts, and berries completely to themselves. The displaced tinier diners are forced to wait glumly on a nearby fence or telephone wire, or hop indecorously about beneath the gluttonous jays pecking at husks and crumbs like paupers at a lordly feast.

From time to time, though, a cadre of Band-tailed Pigeons will make their official appearance in order to survey the backyard scene and restore order where deemed necessary. Now, these aren't your basic downtown park-bench pigeons. Not the scruffy ragamuffins who skitter about in bustling cities panhandling for bread crumbs. No, our country pigeons dress smartly and carry themselves with a highly dignified and authoritative air, in the manner of English officers. Or, more correctly, Confederate generals, their uniform of choice being predominantly gray. These straight-backed, stiff-necked overseers prefer to arrive unannounced and inspect the premises and residents just to keep a proper eye on things. They strut regally about, heads held high, feathers all in place, wings clasped smartly behind their backs, ascertaining that all feeders are in good working order, and that each and every fellow fine feathered fighter is behaving as befits his or her station and rank. Once satisfied of the precise preparedness and fitness of the situation (and once they've eaten their fill), these fine gentlemen will bestow a snappy salute and make winged haste for the lush confines of the neighbor's barn, where they presumably compare notes, formulate battle plans, and sip Earl Grey Tea.

The Steller's Jays are nowhere to be seen when the brigadier pigeons come calling. Layabout dilettantes and scalawags that they are, the Jays fully realize they would never pass inspection, especially when it comes to genteel conduct.

Then of course, you have your darling doves, cute little pudgy balls of feathers, scurrying around in pairs and packs along the garden pathways, exchanging all the latest gossip gleaned from the migratory swallows, robins and hummingbirds as they come and go from strange and faraway climes.

Said swallows tend to keep to themselves, though, laying claim to the aforementioned telephone lines when they breeze into town, swooping and flocking like schools of feathered fish. We like swallows in Bucolia. They like to eat mosquitoes. We don't like mosquitoes. Not one bit. Swoop on, o hungry swallows, and chomp the flock out of them nasty bloodsuckers!

And, of course, robins are the harbingers of spring. We greet them in Bucolia with much pomp, circumstance, and offering up of worms and bugs. They trill so sweetly, with their chests so red, what's not to like? The Steller's Jays, on the other hand, will be singing gloriously one minute, then squawking up an ungodly racket the next. Very contradictory and ill mannered, those Steller's Jays.

But the favorite of many of us hinterfolk would have to be the hummingbird. Starting and stopping on a dime, as though Mother Nature had them wired into her very own remote control and just couldn't stop fiddling with the fast-forward and stop buttons, they're real charmers. Unique in color and motion, you could watch those hummers for hours on end as they zip about from flower to feeder and back again. Trouble is, their aerial performances generally only last a few seconds. You gotta have a quick eye when it comes to hummingbird viewing. Want a close encounter of the hummingbird kind? Just wear some red and sit very, very still. Soon you'll hear that telltale hummbuzz in your ear. Roll your eyes slowly sideways and you'll likely catch the little guy giving you an assessing look: "Is this one sweet enough to eat? Nah!" And off he'll buzz.

Speaking of buzzing off...

One warm day—it might have been during our second summer in Bucolia—Donna and I were relaxing in our living room, taking a break from the day's grueling gardening, gazing raptly out the window where seemingly all the birds in the 'hood were chowing down at the banquet of feeders, worms, and bugs. We looked away for a moment, exchanging one of those isn't-it-amazing-we're-so-blessed-to-live-in-a-natural-wonderland-like-this glances with each other, and when we looked back out the window, we were stunned.

Every single bird was gone. Vanished. Just like that. We sat there in stupefied and squinty-eyed puzzlement, until something plunged precipitously out of the sky and onto our backyard fence. What came to rest there, talons clutching wood fencepost, was a Red-tailed

Hawk. Turns out that every feaster at our backyard banquet lost their appetite when they realized they might become someone else's feast. Even the arrogant Steller's Jay. Seems that even bullies can be bullied.

We're rarely treated to such raptor visits in the confines of our yard, and it's an awesome moment when they do occur. And I do mean "moment," since they generally hang around on a fencepost about as long as hummingbirds will hover while inspecting Donna's red earrings. Unless there's something tasty nearby. Oh sure, we can always find stately creatures soaring and coasting high up in the country sky. But at that distance, it's hard to tell a bald eagle from a turkey vulture. Up close though, when you can really see the fluff and color of their fantastic feathers, sense the sheer predatory power of their beaks and talons, and practically stare into their searching eye, that's a delight —no, an honor I'd say—that's hard to forget.

Speaking of raptors, owls, who work the night shift, love to spend time in our woods. We rarely see them, but their distinctive calls echo throughout the valley. When I first heard them, I thought someone was pulling my leg. Or tugging my wing. Whatever. The hooting was so loud and clear that I assumed some prankster had hiked up into the trees, determined to pull one over on the newcomers. But the hooting persisted from night to night, moved from spot to spot, and from time to time was answered by responding calls from down the road and across the valley. Either these pranksters had way too much time on their hands, or we were indeed being serenaded by winged denizens of the night.

Donna and I consulted our growing library of bird-related books and determined our elusive yet vociferous residents were of the Barred Owl variety. Soon, I found myself imitating their call, and incredibly, they began responding. Some nights, we'll carry on long, drawn-out conversations. What are we talking about? Whooooo knows? Probably they just find me a source of great amusement: "Get a load of that wingless wonder wandering around outside his nest hooting his darn fool head off. Call Olaf and Olivia from up in the north wood. They've gotta see this! Things have gotten a whole lot more entertaining around here since that buffoon brought his roost over the mountain."

It can be also quite entertaining—for us humans—when early summer rolls around. Eggs hatch and tiny little fluffs of wing and beak begin poking their heads out from under rafters, eaves, and bushes. Mind you, it's not so entertaining for the momma birds involved. Like any infants, the winged varieties are extremely needy and suffer severely from separation anxiety. Moms are constantly being harassed and chased around by their insistent offspring, creating quite the spectacle amongst garden bushes and trees. The younguns are eager to try out their new wings, but not so eager to be out of eyesight of their parents. Hence, a sort of fluttering version of hide-and-seek or tag ensues. And the mommas always, and quite reluctantly, seem to be "It."

The most prominent players of this game are ravens. Mom and pop will fly and glide back and forth from one set of woods to another, with their sons and daughters in hot pursuit. All will be loudly exclaiming, "Brrraaawwk! Brrraaawwk! Brrraaawwk!" the entire time. Quite the aerial display accompanied by a cacophonous symphony. Of course, yours truly feels to compel to chat with the ravens as well. You'd think a political convention was taking place, what with all the shouting and going round in circles. It's no wonder the owls tend to vacate the woods during this time of year. Who wants to live amid all that racket?

Who, indeed, but someone who fancies himself a bird-talker.

Still, I sure would like to catch another glimpse of those Sandhill Cranes. Or maybe they were Great Blue Herons. How should I know? I can't tell a bull from a heifer.

Matthew Thuney

Chapter 9: Livin' in the Land of the Truncated Gerund

Far be it from me to say that Bucolia has its own language. Folks in these parts speak American just fine, thank you. But I reckon there is a sort of dialect that takes some getting used to.

For one thing, I'm pretty darn sure you can be fined for ending any word with a G. Maybe I should have said, "Endin' a word with a G." But let's dispense with the idea of conversational penalties for the time bein' and continue with our linguistic scrutiny of the bucolic tongue.

In Bucolia, for instance, a whole lot of fishin' and huntin' goes on. Or at least a whole lot of fishin' and huntin' gets talked about. It's hard to tell exactly how much really happens. You come across a shady bend in a nice runnin' river or creek (sorry, *crick*), and some Bucolian is likely to lament how he wishes he had his fishin' pole. That lament will be followed by a blow-by-blow description of how the fella once netted a 27-pound salmon in that very spot. Or maybe another spot just like that. Or maybe it was a 12-pound trout. Somethin' like that, anyways. And it sure put up one hell of a fight!

When it comes to huntin' stories, yours truly is not so inclined to listen. On account of I find fishin' at least somewhat sportly: the contest of wits and wills between cunning caster and wily swimmer; the summoning up of proper bait; the search for the perfect combination of light, shade, depth; the guzzling of countless brews. It's a kind of a dance really, or maybe a bit of a stagger, twixt man above and fish below. A true contest of wits and wills. One I generally come out on the short end of, as you might imagine, but that just possibly could culminate in a fresh and tasty meal. Or, more likely, a trip to the local fishmonger.

But huntin'? I must confess I just don't get it. Oh sure, I've heard the wild and woolly tales of trackin' the prey, waitin' patiently for just the right moment to site and strike. And I've heard tell of folks who honestly do hunt for food. I guess you gotta do what you gotta do; but I don't guess I gotta admire it. There's just somethin' about somebody with a weapon hidin' behind a bush or up a tree, takin' aim at some animal a-way over yonder, shootin' some sort of projectile at it—be it bullet or arrow—and claimin' it's a fair fight. That seem fair to you? I must be missin' somethin'. Wouldn't be the first time!

Nonetheless—and I'll dispense with the truncated Bucolia-speak for now, lest you need an expert translator or maybe even subtitles—there is an endearing quality to the lingo of the countryside. It's real; it's immediate. Most of all, it doesn't lend itself to misunderstanding the way some dialects do. Take for example what we used to refer to as "Valley Girl" talk, but now passes for common parlance among many segments of younger society.

Like, when it seems like every statement ends in a question? You know? Like maybe I think you might not understand what I'm saying? Or, you know, like maybe *I* don't understand what I'm saying? So if I finish off every bit of conversation with a rising tone of voice, maybe you won't question me or even think about what I'm saying? Because I'm not sure if you're not sure, you know? So we can all, you know, not be sure together and not make any real statements or draw any conclusions at all?

Here in Bucolia, we rarely walk away from a conversation thinking, "What the hell was that all about?" Sure, we might come away thinking, "I've never heard so much bovine manure come out of one person's mouth before," but there may be some wisdom amongst all the cow pies. Even when it's someone like me doing the talking. And we generally have fun spreading conversational compost and picking through the clumps for the occasional gold nugget.

Lest you think that Bucolese has primarily detracted from the English language (most notably excising the aforementioned G's), this unique dialect has also increased usage of certain words in turn. Shining examples might be the words "at," "them," and "seen." Well, maybe not *shining*, per se.

Around, oh, the mid-1980's, that tiny two-letter powerhouse "at" suddenly surged from the rear of the prepositional pack to the very front. This mysterious renaissance can only be attributed to the resurgence of country lingo right about that time. It was cool to be country in the Eighties, with singers like Clint Black, Garth Brooks, and Reba McIntyre all over the Top 40 charts and grinnin' and pickin' on prime time TV. Country was where it was at. Ah, and there's that word!

Pretty soon, "at" was where it was at. "At" seemed to be completing every other sentence. It was no longer enough to tell someone where you were. You now had to tell them where you were *at*. As in this typical phone conversation…

"Hey, Bubba, where you at?"

"I'm to home, dummy. Dincha just call my home number?"

"Thought you'd be down the bar by now."

"That where you at?"

"Damn straight that's where I'm at."

"Well sit tight and have a cold one waitin' fer me."

"That's where it's at, bro."

And so on. Moreover, those two dudes were likely employees at Microsoft in 1986 holding stock in hot commodities like The Gap and Reebok.

Then there's "them," which continues to shove poor disused "those" aside to this very day here in Bucolia. As in, "Look at them cute little fillies down the end of the bar. They sure are pretty. Let's go chat 'em up some."

For added emphasis, "there" is often added to "them." To wit: "Hell, dumbass, them there ain't no fillies. Them there's colts all gussied up like fillies. You sure we're in the right bar?"

"Truth be told, I ain't quite certain where we're at. Best pour us another one, barkeep. Might improve our eyesight."

So "them" replaces "those" just as "seen" replaces "saw." Hence our little barroom scene might climax thusly:

"Why don't you just wander on down there and give them filly-colts the once over, see if you can figger 'em out."

"Hell, you seen 'em first. You go."

Thirty-seven seconds later…

"Well I checked 'em out, and I don't like what I seen. Fact is, I'm a bit corn-fused. They both done got boy-bumps in the middle of their throats like you and me. You know, your basic Adam's Apples? Ain't that what the Good Lord intended just for male types?"

"How do you know what the Good Lord intended? You ain't been to church in nigh on a month of Sundays. Besides, this here's the 1980's. Let's just mosey on down there and have us a parley. Might learn somethin'. Maybe even have a few laughs. Them two seem friendly enough. Don't know 'bout you, but I could use the company. Barkeep, would you be so kind as to send them there two gentle-ladies a beer on us? I believe we're about to have us one hell of an interestin' evenin'."

To which the bartender replies, "That's where it's at, boys. That's where it's at."

Now, you might recoil in horror at how country folk mangle the King's English. And I, having spent much of my life learning and implementing proper grammar and usage, might be inclined to join you in said recoil. However, you have to admit, it's not just the flora and fauna that are colorful in Bucolia. A good part of its charm and

85

spirit comes from the two-legged characters that inhabit it. And how those characters, shall we say, conversify with one another.

Conversifyin' 'bout Critters and Dinner

It's not just how Bucolians speak that sets them apart, though. It's also the topics they tend to favor. Primarily (and this should come as no great surprise) animals and food.

The fact that cows play a central role in country life, much to my chagrin, has already been discussed and established. However, there are other critters afield, most notably horses, pigs, sheep, goats, and even llamas and alpacas. And dogs. Everywhere, dogs.

You probably won't be shocked to learn that yours truly has difficulty telling sheep from goats. But our neighbor up the road has some sheep and goats that need grazing land, and we have some open pasture to offer, so I'm definitely headed for a crash course in wool versus hair, manes versus horns, that sort of thing.

Regarding llamas and alpacas, I'm not even sure their owners can tell the difference. Except maybe one has a longer neck and the other spits farther.

Pigs you just don't see a whole lot of out in the open. It's not like they graze majestically in roadside fields. No, when it comes to pigs you pretty much have to go visit them in their pens. Which is not high on my bucolic to-do list. They tell me pigs are quite intelligent, actually very clean animals. You'd be hard put to convince me of that. I mean, where do you think the word *sloppy* came from? What animal absolutely defines the word *wallow*? And why do you suppose Charles Schulz named his most hygienically challenged Peanuts character Pigpen?

Horses, on the other hand, are, well, a horse of a different color. Supposedly, horses aren't the sharpest needle in the haystack, but come on now, horses just look regal. Not to mention pretty as all get-out. Even the most sway-backed old mare remains possessed of a certain dignity.

A couple of summers ago, our nearby neighbor pastured some horses for a friend. It was such a pleasure gazing at them as they pranced, galloped, chased each other around. Just watching them be horses made me want to don a ten-gallon hat, kick back on the porch with my feet propped up, munching on a piece of hay. Thankfully I refrained. I never would've heard the end of it from genuine buckaroos up and down our valley. Sadly, our horse-sitting neighbors, who had day jobs and plenty to do in town during off hours, soon realized that feeding and looking after horses was far less fun than watching them gallivant about. That former horse pasture is now a very nice hay field. Which is kind of a shame, because I was just on the verge of learning the difference between a pony, a colt, and a filly.

By and large, though, Bucolia has gone to the dogs. It must be some sort of unwritten rule that if you farm, you are required to have a dog. Naturally, Donna and I have cats. Two cats. Well, two and a half if you count the stray black Siamese blend who adopted us some time ago. We call that one Maow. At least, that's what she told me when I inquired as to her name: "Maow," she clearly replied. Maow is extremely talkative and especially delights in saying her own name over and over with different nuances and inflections. I reply in kind, and we seem to understand one another quite well. True, most of our conversations involve food, but we'll occasionally chat about the weather or exchange gossip about the neighborhood birds. Which also often wind up as food for Maow, come to think of it.

Our two house cats, Karma and Neo, are studies in opposites. Karma is the lovable, sad-eyed scruffian; Neo the aristocratic, above-it-all noblynose. I say "house cats" because *we* live in *their* house and should feel privileged to see to their needs. Lord Neo in particular makes that abundantly clear.

However, Donna and I are definitely in the minority as cat owners. In fact, folks around here look at us funny for not having a dog around. Thing is, we do have dogs around. They just aren't our dogs. Seems as though every dog in the neighborhood likes to visit our garden, porch, and deck. From the Rhodesian Ridgeback across the way to the English Sheepdog way down at the end of the road, they all like to stop by, assisting us with their highly developed digging skills and helping themselves to Maow's leftovers. And I must admit that dogs are far superior to cats when it comes to keeping unwanted bigger critters—coyotes, mostly—at bay. On the other hand, Maow does a pretty darn good job at keeping the gangs of mice, moles, and voles under control, judging by the bits of skull, tails, and feet she thoughtfully leaves as tribute on our back porch. Thanks, Maow.

Which brings us back to food. Of the human kind. And when to eat what. This distinction manifested itself even before Donna and I moved out to Bucolia. When we lived in town and Donna's family dwelled a-way out in the county, we would often invite them over for dinner. Imagine our surprise when the family showed up at one o'clock in the afternoon! Did they live in a different time zone? Or perhaps they just enjoyed our company and wanted to spend a few extra hours with us. But no, they expected to be fed right then and there. It was, after all, dinnertime, dadgum it!

Turns out that what we city folk call lunch, country folk call dinner. And what we city folk call dinner, country folk call supper. When you're raised on a farm, dinner is the day's big meal, and it takes place in the early afternoon following the morning chores. Supper is a lesser repast you snack on after all the day's work is done and you're about ready to turn in for the night. Breakfast is a biggie, too. Gets you ready for the day. Lunch apparently does not exist. It's just something we city folk conjured up for no good reason at all. No wonder we're fatter than farmers. We haven't got the good sense to know what to eat or when to eat it.

And how much exercise can you get trying to walk or play fetch with a cat?

Chapter 10: A Busy Day on the Road

Living as we do at the very edge of the known universe, you wouldn't think there'd be much in the way of traffic here in Bucolia. Not much to slow you down or impede your progress in getting from one point to another. Especially considering how far apart the one point might be from the other out here where distances seem to be miraculously stretched by the hand of a mythical giant. Still, you'd be surprised. Some days it can indeed take quite awhile to get from point A to point B, even on the paved roads.

Part of the problem is that, unlike the city and many suburbs, our roads are used for more than just driving. Driving cars, I mean. You find some awfully funny-looking vehicles on the highways and byways out here, and they tend to drive slow. Really slow.

And it's not just tractors, although we have our lion's share of those chugging along. Especially during plowing and haying seasons when tractors are as ubiquitous as school buses. The tractors might not stop as often as the buses do, but they tend to proceed at a snail's pace, so the effect is about the same. Plan to run a little late if you're on the road when kids are going to and from school. Plan to run a lot late when it's plowing or haying season. You just get used to it. Besides, tractors are generally easy to get around, since there's hardly ever much traffic coming the opposite direction. And bucolic tractor drivers are pretty savvy. They'll ride the shoulder and wave you around when it's safe to pass. Unless you're some impatiently belligerent city slicker who insists on riding their tail and weaving all over kingdom come. Then your friendly bucolic tractor driver might just wait until a nice, big semi is coming in the other direction before giving you the go-ahead.

So be prepared to spend a little extra time on the road while farmers are preparing their fields or cutting their hay. But harvest time? That's when you'll be treated to some truly odd sights.

Come harvest time, the roads of Bucolia play host to all manner of strange and menacing machines. It's like a scene out of *Road Warrior* or a showcase for weird weaponry the Borg from *Star Trek* might invent. You'll be cruising on down the highway when all of a sudden you come upon a seemingly random collection of metal, spikes, and blades all piled on top of a set of wheels. A *huge* collection of metal, spikes, and blades on top of cartoonishly *humongous* wheels. Glistening, menacing thrashers and chompers propelled by tires the size of a Volkswagen Beetle. In fact, I'm pretty sure I saw a Volkswagen Beetle stuck in one of these monster's treads last fall. And atop this mass of monstrous metal—or somewhere lodged in the middle like a fly caught in amber—will be a tiny cage bearing a hunched-over operator grinning maniacally beneath his weather-beaten John Deere cap.

"Oh Lord," you'll pray, "Please don't let that thing loose on my house. Or garden. Or cats. Well, maybe the cats; they've been more uppity than usual lately. Please, Lord, just don't let it be me."

Later on, you'll be driving past a field or orchard and there will be that doggone machine, all unfurled from its embryonic traveling state and doing what it was invented to do: harvest corn, pick berries, whatever needs to be done that makes your kitchen a simpler, tastier place to make a meal. Then you'll realize that *you've* slowed to a crawl, mesmerized by the machine's progress, and a whole line of cars is stacking up behind *you*. You've turned into the Greenhorn Gawker: another roadway hazard in Bucolia.

Still, it's more than machinery that causes traffic delays in the hinterlands. It's people. Because, we the people of Bucolia like to use our roads for activities other than driving. Such as, of all things, walking.

So you'll need to allow a few extra minutes travel time on sunny afternoons as well. Because, every quarter mile or so you must be prepared to perform what you might call the Roadside Skootch. As you're driving on your merry way, if the road is warm and dry—or at least not running with rain or covered in ice—you're bound to run into a neighbor or three walking the road. Why would they do such an inconvenient, anachronistic thing? Because this is Bucolia. It's beautiful around here, why wouldn't you want to go for a leisurely stroll on a nice day, enjoy the fresh air, the panoramic vistas, the endless, ever-changing sky, take advantage of the chance to flag down a neighbor as they drive by. So you all crowd over to the shoulder doing that good ol' Roadside Skootch.

You could say that talking to neighbors while they walk the road is Bucolia's version of CNN. It's the best way to get all the news. And the gossip. We in the boondocks are definitely not immune to gossip. In fact, we thrive on it. We positively relish finding out what folks across the valley might—or might not—be up to. Usually, it must be said, gossip hereabouts isn't nearly as juicy as the scandalous skullduggery one is accustomed to in the Big City. So we have to make up for our lack of quantity with, well, lack of quality it would seem. Instead of going on about which Hollywood starlet is cheating on which star, we country dwellers will shake our heads over how noted baker Mrs. Lumply overcooked her famous gooseberry pie, thus disappointing the gathering at the Potternost family picnic. Or we'll gasp in dismay about how farmer Cutterson prematurely harvested his feed corn, thereby angering cattle ranchers up and down the valley and causing consternation among dissatisfied cows and pigs alike. We take our food seriously around here, after all, both animals *and* humans.

Or you might slow your pickup down to chat with an acquaintance clip-clopping along the side of the road on horseback. This can prove tricky, as not all horses are amenable to the machinations of motorized vehicles. Best just wave hello and move on down the road for safety's sake.

Other animals aren't so circumspect about traversing country roads, though. In Bucolia, it's wise to exercise your powers of peripheral vision. You never know when some deer will high-tail it out of the underbrush, some goat will decide it's a fine day to jump the fence and try to hitch a ride, some friendly pooch will figure he can outrace your Camry, or some possum will try to accomplish the impossible dream (you know, to cross the road).

Or you might even have a chance encounter with Pam the Pig who dwells down the road. Pam's easy to recognize—she's the one with the bandana tied fashionably around her neck. Good luck getting around her, though. Pam's gambit is to stop right in front of your vehicle and demand that you come out and chat with her. I suppose it's only mannerly to do so. Moreover, trust me, blowing your horn will do no good. Pam clearly does not countenance such loud, unseemly, disturbing displays, and simply will not be moved by them. Why, the very idea…how rude!

So whether you're a denizen of Bucolia or just passing through, it's a good idea to keep your eyes peeled and allow a little extra time to get from here to there. You're on country time now. Clocks tick a little more slowly around here.

Chapter 11: The Sound and the Fury…

Remember all those confessions I promised to make earlier? Well, here's a big one: all is not always sweetness and light here in Bucolia. We have our sour, dark days as well. On second thought, maybe not so sour, but bitter in the sense of cold. And most definitely dark. Or at least hazy. With great streaks of flashing light thrown in for good measure.

Because Mama Nature, with all her splendorous bounty, color, and life, like everyone has her bad days. At least, less than pleasant days for us comfort-loving humans. There are indeed downsides to living far from the densely packed communities of cities and towns, away from the temperate influence of oceans and bays. Inland valleys and rolling foothills, picturesque as they may be, can play host to some of Mama's more spectacular and unnerving displays of pique. Moreover, when those piques are displayed, the idea of isolation tends to lose its sense of romanticism, sort of like a blind date winding up with a hike to a bat cave.

The very first week Donna and I spent in our freshly-dragged-over-the mountain home, we were treated to a wildly unexpected occurrence. And I'm not referring to the Jehovah's Witnesses showing up at our front door. But, come to think of it, how in the heck did they find us even way out here? One dedicated and well-travelled group, those JW's, you gotta give 'em that.

No, this was an unexpected occurrence of the meteorological kind. We hadn't yet signed up to pay a massive amount for satellite and internet service yet—it took longer for those vultures to find us than it did the Witnesses—so we were without forewarning. Moreover, the field surrounding the newly embedded house was a bulldozed mass of dirt—so we were without the fundamental protection of grass and shrub.

Donna and I were inside unpacking boxes, marveling at our new abode, wondering how on earth we had crammed so much crap into our previous two-bedroom apartment and how on earth we were going to fit everything into our new quarters over twice that size, when we noticed the sky begin to darken. Clouds were rolling in. Big, roiling, sinister clouds.

"Ooh," exclaimed Donna, who had been raised in this valley, "This is wonderful! You've never experienced a thunderstorm here before. Judging by those clouds, you're in for a real treat!"

Now, I've always been a big admirer of thunder and lightning. Probably due in no small measure to my mother's ministrations when I was a child. At night, when the heavens began to rumble and I pulled my covers tight to my chin, my mom would visit my bedroom with the assurance, "That's just God up there bowling." When the first flash of lightning would light up my window, she'd say, "Wow, that must have been a strike!" I've been fascinated by thunderstorms ever since. Though I never did take to bowling. Not nearly as exciting. Just loud, with strange shoes.

So, with the promise of an enhanced thunderstorm experience playing in my mind, Donna and I donned our barn boots (dirt boots, to be more precise, since we were barnless at the time, yet blessed with an abundance of dirt) and headed out to what was loosely referred to as our back yard, which more closely resembled an Oklahoma wheat field during the height of the Dust Bowl era: a bunch of hardpan with some sprigs of yellowish stuff trying desperately to make a go of it.

Standing there in our alleged back yard bordered by our wooded hillside on the west and matching (and, it turned out, conspiring) hills across the river to the east, gazing up at the quickly moving skyscape which for all the world looked somewhat like a series of misshapen gray and black bowling balls perhaps designed by Salvador Dali, we were indeed treated to a show of shows. It began with the sound, a distant, ominous rumble emanating from somewhere to the south. As the rumbling marched northward, sort of like Lee toward Gettysburg, I half expected it to be accompanied by a Wagnerian soundtrack. But no, the soundtrack that soon burst upon us proved far more magnificent. And the ensuing battle proved far more effective than Pickett's charge.

Donna had tried to describe to me what a thunderstorm in the valley sounds like; the way the noise rumbles slowly between the hills. However, as I stood there and the storm shouldered its way into our very own dale, all Donna's attempts at verbal description were washed away. When the first peel of thunder broke over our heads, I actually physically ducked. The mammoth booming was so loud, so protracted, that for one crazy instant I feared the heavens might crash right down upon me. And the echoing rumble that followed, bouncing deafeningly between the hills, seemed endless. With each crash, I ducked and dodged, as if one puny human could hope to escape this mad bowling alley of the gods.

Lightning followed the noisy vanguard, bringing even more thunder with it. God must have been really on his game that day, because the light show we witnessed indicated an extremely high score. Whole sections of the sky lit up brilliantly, shockingly as it were. Every now and then a streak would dash forth, charging down toward the valley, pointing its brilliant sword tip ominously at hills, trees, barns, and homes. And there we stood, tiny and unnoticed as ants under a herd of elephants. Not red ants or flying ants, either. We couldn't sting back or zoom away. Just had to remain there, rooted to the earth, in gaping awe. Moments like that give one pause to think about one's place in the cosmos, and how that place might not be quite as significant as one had previously assumed.

The next moments gave us pause to think about whether we, or our new home, would even survive this humbling display of divine bowling or elephantine stampeding. For, now, the heavens opened up. And it didn't just rain, it gushed water. Someone had opened the Great Fire Hydrant in the Sky, and we were standing directly under it.

Apart from being stupefied and drenched, Donna and I now found ourselves awash in a quagmire of mud. Our awestruck admiration of the storm quickly dissolved into sheer panic, as it seemed as though our back yard would swiftly be swept away and the house itself just might be next. Gasping for air—the rain fell so heavily that it seemed like we were swimming through waves—we grabbed a couple of shovels and began furiously digging a trench to lead what was becoming a swiftly flowing canal away from the house. Donna and I must have resembled Mel Gibson and Sissy Spacek from *The River* at this point. Though I suspect the more experienced Donna was playing more the Mel and I, flailing wildly about, more the Sissy.

Miraculously, we were spared being washed away when the rain quickly subsided and the storm made its mighty way northward rumbling fiercely as it went. Sopping wet and covered in mud, Donna and I had little to show for our savage encounter with Mother Nature except for a crudely dug ditch that continued to siphon off the remaining rivulets of water from drain spouts and hardpan.

The next storm, however, this one of the windy variety, would claim as its victim my beloved barbeque, which was blown over and tossed around like a tin cup, lid, legs, and racks strewn about as if attacked by flying monkeys. Nonetheless, I was able to respond with an unprecedented display of screwdriver and wrench, thus prolonging the life of my steak-burning friend for another couple of summers. I know, I know, you're thinking in disbelief, Matt actually *fixed* something? Nevertheless, it's true, dear reader, it's true. I dug down deep, and from some heretofore-untapped reservoir where the handyman in each of us dwells, even writers, I summoned the gods of metal, fire, and grease, and managed to save that storm-tossed grill. Hallelujah, Carnivore Kingdom!

Then I covered that sucker with an industrial strength tarp, tied up the ends, and weighted it down with brick and stone. Because that's what you learn to do with outdoor equipment in Bucolia: cover it, tie it up, weight it down. Then hope you never have to use it again, on account of it'll take you an entire morning just to unwrap the doggone thing.

If the thunderstorms and raging winds in these parts are amazingly majestic and powerfully chaotic, the fog, in its unique way, is eerily mysterious. Fog seems to travel the valley along the edges of the river like a horde of ghostly boatmen. You never know when you'll wake up in the morning to a world so obscure that you'll need to check your clock. Is it morning? Or maybe afternoon? Has the outside world simply vanished, and your home whisked away in the night to some alien dimension? Will Rod Serling, Jean-Luc Picard, or perhaps Gandalf step through your bedroom door and welcome you to a new realm?

Your sense of space will be clouded, too. Okay, you've risen, prepared yourself; you're ready to start the day. Hop in your car, but wait: where did the road go? It must be down at the end of the driveway somewhere. Maybe the ghostly boatmen carried the road off as booty to be bartered in some land down the river where asphalt is a highly prized treasure. Or the aliens or elves decided, "Roads? We don't need no stinkin' roads," and beamed the thoroughfare into oblivion.

So you slowly inch your way forward until you spy a white line, and follow that magical guide for all it's worth, praising for once in your life the beleaguered county workers who put it there. But once you reach that infamous bucolic one-lane river bridge...presto! The fog lifts, the sun tries to peer down at you but looks more like the moon, then, boom! Back into the gloom as you approach the Great Highway into Town. Looks like the ghostly boatmen, aliens, and elves have decided to pillage the roads on the other side of the river as well.

And so it goes. Fog...light! Fog...light! Fog...light! Until you reach the border of Bucolia, beyond which the ghostly boatmen fear to go.

And we Bucolians wouldn't have it any other way. The all-embracing fog, when it comes, is welcome as is the thunder, lightning, wind and rain. It wouldn't be Bucolia without the challenges Mama Nature throws our way. Challenges? Not so much. Gifts, that's what we consider the meteorological oddities out here. True, they're the kind of gifts your weird uncle might bring you during the holidays. Nevertheless, you love your weird uncle and the strange gifts he comes up with. And we Bucolians love Mother Nature. We pretty much have to, considering our lives depend upon Her bounty and goodness. We can deal with the tantrums and scoldings. After all, we're just kids.

...And the Three Stooges

There is one gift from our Mama that some of us, in keeping with the holiday spirit, would honestly like to return, though. That gift is winter.

Me? I like snow. No, I love snow. However, that sentiment is not, shall we say, universally shared out here in the country. For instance, some folks don't seem to share my fondness for driving in the snow. I can't imagine why. Just flip on the defroster, crank up the heat, engage the four-wheel drive, and start humming some holiday tunes…you're in a winter wonderland! Plowing slowly through the snowy roads like a modern-day sleigh, windshield wipers merrily flapping the softly falling flakes away. What could possibly be more bucolic in a wintry way?

Sadly, it's not all softly falling flakes and four-wheel-drive. Sometimes winter is just plain friggin' cold, windy, and icy. Hard to feel all warm and fuzzy about cold and icy. Even I have a hard time humming holiday tunes twixt chattering teeth.

And there's one minor detail I haven't mentioned about Bucolia, which is this: we tend to lose power from time to time. And by "from time to time," I mean don't bother to reset the clocks on your ovens, coffee makers and radios from roughly November 1 to March 31. It's just not worth the constant effort. And be sure to have the regional electric company on your cell phone's speed dial. And be sure to wave at the ever-present utility crews, offer them a cup of coffee, get to know them by name. They'll be your best friends every winter.

Oh, it's not just wintertime that the power goes out here. A stray leaf, errant raindrop, or overweight swallow could just as easily do the trick. You never know when you'll wake up or come home to a dark house. And, in a place where even the water from your well is pumped by electricity, things can get gamey pretty quick.

But it was one winter in particular—possibly our first, having tried to block the traumatic memory from my mind, I cannot be sure—that Donna and I discovered that a bucolic winter was nothing to trifle with.

I do recall awakening that ominous morning to a cold bedroom. Cold, as in you don't want to get out from under the covers lest you discover your bedroom rug is a frozen mass of unyielding fibers beneath your bare feet cold. Cold, as in why am I seeing my breath cold. I stared blankly at the bedside digital clock, which, numberless and numb, stared blankly back at me. Even I was smart enough to figure out what that meant.

"Donna," I said, nudging my still-sleeping wife, "we've lost power again."

"Fine," she mumbled, "Just go back to sleep."

"No," I whispered, "You don't understand. The house is cold."

"Just stay under the covers. Let me sleep a little more."

"I mean it's *really* cold," I whined. Then I struck upon a grand idea. The hand with which I had nudged Donna lay atop the blanket like a frozen tilapia filet. I reached over, drew down her share of the blanket, and touched her now bare shoulder with my flash-frozen fishstick hand.

"Holy crap!" she exclaimed, suddenly wide-awake. "It's cold! There's no heat! What happened?!"

"The electricity's out. Again. Only this time it's somewhat chilly outside. Inside, too, come to think of it. Do you think maybe we should start the generator?"

"Good idea," Donna agreed, as we both shot out of bed and rapidly donned several layers of clothing. Cold clothing.

Now here's the deal. We had recently purchased a generator, a used one, from Donna's brother who hadn't started it in years and had no need of it. Like good citizens of Bucolia, we had dragged the heavy hunk of machinery into town and gotten it all tuned up and ready to go.

Thing is, we had never actually used the generator before. Had never actually used *any* generator before. Had no owner's manual. Had no clue. So we wheeled it out of a shed and stood there looking dumbly down at it, freezing to death.

There was a long, thick coil of a power cord curled on top of the mysterious machine. This, we vaguely recalled from some long-ago instruction by a fellow Bucolian, needed to be connected from the generator to our utility post. Well, we managed to figure out which prongs went into what openings—it was kind of like sex education for the mechanically challenged—and connections were made. Incredibly, I somehow remembered that a switch in the utility box had to be thrown so that the power from the generator would be directed to our house rather than the rest of the neighborhood.

All that remained to be done was to turn the generator on. Which had switches and toggles and sliding thingies everywhere.

Did I mention it was cold? Really, really cold? As in 9° outside. Probably about 10° inside. So there we were, dancing around, stamping our feet, clapping our hands, removing our gloves and putting them back on as we tried this and that combination of switches and tugged in vain at the pull-start cord (yes, we had forgotten to replace the dead battery). We must for all the world looked like a couple of Eskimos performing an ancient ghost dance as we tried to bring the beast to life.

Then, magically, as if summoned by our primordial rite, Donna's dad Vernon appeared from nowhere. Our savior, we thought. Vernon will know what to do. And, sure enough, he joined the fray and began by taking one look at the generator, then asking, "Where's the key?" And he gave me that look out from under his John Deere cap that seemed to say, "For a guy who went to college, you sure don't know much." He's given me that look more than once. More than 16 times, it's fair to estimate.

Rallying to my own defense, I offered indignantly, "What key? There is no key."

Vernon glared at me, said nothing, and jabbed his finger at the spot on the side of silent machine which sported a neat, round circle marked off by three distinct points that clearly said, "OFF, START, ON." The center of the circle featured a neat little serrated slot. Exactly the sort of mechanism into which one might expect to insert a key.

"Oh," I shivered, and made my way into the house, rummaging through a kitchen drawer where we kept all manner of misplaced keys whose purpose had been lost to history. One of them bore a stubby little knob on one end, clearly marked "Honda." Since the generator was the only piece of Honda equipment we owned, I cleverly deduced that that could be the missing key. Let's see a non-college-educated guy figure that one out!

Triumphantly, I returned to the chaotic scene in our back yard and thrust the key at Vernon, who shook is head, grabbed it, and shoved it into the slot. He turned the key to the ON position (I could've figured that out, too!), then commenced yanking for all he was worth on the doggone pull cord. He yanked and yanked and yanked some more.

Nothing. Not a shudder, nary a gasp, nor even a sigh emanated from the dastardly device. The generator sat there like a block of lifeless metal, stone, or ice. Which was exactly what we were all turning into.

So we all commenced to flipping switches, sliding thingies, poking, prodding, checking repeatedly that there was indeed gas in the varmint. With three sets of hands now fluttering this way and that over the truculent beast in the grey-white cold of the wintry morning, clouds of frustrated breath filling the air, the casual observer would have thought he was witnessing rare footage of an old Buster Keaton comedy. Or, more likely, the Three Stooges.

Because there was a soundtrack of sorts, mostly monosyllabic grunts of surprise and dismay. Such as: "Here! No. This! Dang. Got it! Huh?

There! What? Oh! Nope. Down? Up? Left! Right! Son-of-a! Gas? Yep. Nothin'." Lots of nothin'.

At one point, while I was bent over the recalcitrant beast, fiddling with something or other, Vernon gave the pull-cord one final mighty tug. His flying elbow darn near decapitated me, sending my beloved Mariners cap flying and almost yanking the generator bow over stern. Nothing. Still nothing.

One of us made sure the key was switched to START. Another found the gas toggle and flipped it to ON. A third discovered the choke and pulled it OUT. Finally, Vernon rounded on the machine, reached down with great deliberation, and pulled smoothly on the cord. The opening strains of "Also Sprach Zarathustra" filled the chilly air as the generator roared to life.

We were saved.

Not so fast.

After a minute or two, the generator began to hiccup, then sputter, until finally it died. Not enough energy to power the entire monstrosity of a home. Donna made her way to the house's fuse box, commencing another round of flip switching and cord yanking until we discovered the precise combination of elements within the electrical grid that our generator could sustain. The electric furnace was not one of those elements. Thankfully, the pellet stove that we had recently purchased to alleviate our heating bill, was.

And so, power began flowing into our home, restoring it to life, as our pellet stove flickered and moaned, at last issuing forth heat into the cold and dormant living room. There was much rejoicing. And much hurried note taking, as I frantically recreated the arcane series of steps needed to fire up the mystical generator and transferred them from scrawled glove-addled hieroglyphs to the technological safety of my frozen, yet battery-powered, laptop.

Another bucolic lesson learned: As the temperature decreases, so does common sense. At least for the Three Stooges who tried to tackle a simple generator on that fateful day.

Matthew Thuney

Chapter 12: Bucolic Soirees

...And a Bovine Breakout

Life in Bucolia isn't entirely herding cattle, tilling fields, planting, harvesting, or making a lengthy commute into the Big City five days a week. Sure, we work hard, but we like to play, too. In fact, partying in Bucolia can make partying in the Big City look positively pedestrian by comparison.

Out here in the country, we tend to space out our soirees, to line them up with the changing seasons, in order to allow both host and guest maximum preparation and recovery time. Regardless of the occasion, though, the structure of each get-together remains roughly the same.

We begin with sort of a pre-game warm-up. This generally consists of some folks arriving a bit early and helping out with the preparations, whether that be decorating, setting up tables and chairs, last-minute cooking and baking, or simply warming up one's innards with a pre-party sampling of adult beverages.

Then comes the food, and a whole host of folks is likely to show up bearing strange and wonderful dishes. Or at least familiar and fattening ones. These bucolic events are generally potluck, with the emphasis on luck. Donna and I, after several failed attempts to manage who brings what to a gathering, finally figured out that it's much easier just to relax and hope for the best food-wise. It always seemed that, try as we might to assign specific courses or dishes to particular guests—and despite their sincere insistence that they would come through for us with a mouth-watering version of their assigned dish—things rarely turned out as planned. Either the couple who promised to bring the three-bean salad would be unable to attend, or the self-described sous-chef who guaranteed delivery of delectable lasagna turned out to have a very different definition of delectable than everyone else in attendance. It's hard to guarantee anything ahead of time around here during calving season, planting season or harvest season, what with the weather becoming hot and happy or wet and grumpy at a moment's notice. And, town or country, it's impossible to account for differences in taste. Even when it comes to something as seemingly impregnable to culinary malfeasance as lasagna.

So we've learned to embrace the luck of potluck. Which surprisingly often results in an amazing and unexpected array of dishes from old standbys to exotic fare, from appetizers to dessert, from beer can chicken to baked Alaska. On those rare occasions when the vittles are heavy on the salads while light on the pie, or the burgers and dogs are hugely outnumbered by the confections and cake, it really doesn't seem to matter. Folks don't seem to mind that much. True, our hinterland hijinx do tend to revolve mightily around food, but it's not really the food that draws the crowd. It's the crowd that draws the crowd. And, as with the food, it can be hard to plan or predict said crowd. Luck plays as big a part in the makeup of the party as it does the contents of the table.

But I must say that here in Bucolia, when it comes to unpredictable party attendees, the odds are stacked in our favor. Sure, we've suffered the occasional egregiously drunken boor who thinks it's a capital idea to stagger around making lewd comments and bring his evening to a dramatic climax by peeing on a shed or collapsing in a garden. There's sometimes a haughty know-it-all who feels it's her social duty to spread her vast reserves of wisdom to each and every guest as they search desperately for an escape route prior to her approach. Nonetheless, because Bucolians tend to be an unorthodox mix of cultures, tastes, and personalities, we're generally an enjoyable lot who take great pleasure in each other's company. Which is another lucky thing, since some sort of shindig always seems to be simmering out here.

Like life itself, the social scene hereabouts awakens in the spring. Around March and April, it's as though little tendrils of hobnobbery begin reaching out. Seed exchanges at the community hall, planning sessions for upcoming summer festivals, a wedding here, a memorial there. They all, of course, call for food and drink. And they all, of course, call for hugs and gossip.

Then there's what you might call the secret celebration, marked by May Day, or Beltane in the parlance of ancient nature-centered spirituality. It's truly hard to say how many actual Pagans dwell here in Bucolia—it's not a box that's generally checked off on a census form. There are plenty of such nonconformist shindigs to be found if you know where to look. And, man oh man, they can be fun. Or so I'm told. Not that I would know, mind you. Just be advised that a succulent eggplant dish might be more welcome than those juicy Angus burgers you were planning to bring.

But soiree season doesn't officially kick off until Memorial Day weekend. That's when you'll see the first tentative smoke signals from fires stoked by charcoal, propane, and mesquite begin to curl up from back yards throughout the valley. A sure sign that the tastiest time of year has arrived. For humans, at least. For livestock, I reckon it's the scariest time of year. Even for veggies these days, as produce has been finding its way to the grill with increasing frequency as well as delicious results.

Memorial Day soirees tend to be among the more sedate gatherings in Bucolia. Everyone is mostly just relieved to be out and about after a long, hard winter followed by a frenzy of crop planting and animal husbandry. Lots of catching up to do. What have y'all been up to? What are your plans for the summer? Plenty of comfort food and comfortable conversation at the Memorial Day soirees.

Things begin to loosen up in June with Solstice parties and such. The longest day of the year is a big deal in a community based on sunshine and growth, something to celebrate mightily. Summer begins, bringing warm promises and green dreams. A good summer—not too terribly hot, with rain sprinkled in at just the right intervals—means a great harvest. So bring on the good times and hope for the best. Barbeque season is in full swing, which is both a blessing and curse if you're both host and cook. That was one of my personal conundrums during our early days as bucolic party givers.

I do love to grill. But that becomes problematic when a party is breaking out all around you, in your very own back yard, and there you are, tongs lashed to one hand, a spatula permanently attached to the other, hunched over the grill while the merriment bubbles all around you. It even impinges on your ability to imbibe the fruit of the vine, which is an outrage of the worst kind.

On one such occasion, just when there seemed to be a break in the feeding frenzy so that I could fill a plate of my own, I backed cautiously away from the barby, turning slowly around, only to find a whole new swarm of guests spilling off our porch into our yard. It seems the conclave down the road—a happy, healthy, alternative living crew—had belatedly decided to accept our invitation, bearing all sorts of surprising compotes and casseroles. It warmed my heart, and I couldn't help but smile wearily. We hadn't met most of these folks before, and I felt honored that they would join us. Quickly, I grabbed the nearest, fullest bottle of Merlot I could find, and returned to my station at the grill with renewed purpose. Not to mention a welcome opportunity to use up those veggie burgers we had bought.

A little later, with all the grillables grilled and tongs and spatula hung safely on their hooks, I began to trudge tiredly toward the house. Wait...where was that wonderful music coming from? Had someone located the remote control and fired up our stereo? No, I puzzled, that sounds way better than our stereo, even in Hi Def mode. I crept up the porch and peeked inside, amazed to find that a concert had broken out in our dining room! A young couple had set up shop with a fiddle and bass and was playing some of the sweetest Bluegrass music I ever heard. I fixed myself a plate of leftovers, pulled up a chair, made myself comfortable, and was quite likely at that very moment in time the happiest, most content human being on the face of the Earth. Thank you, Bucolia, for yet another amazing surprise.

By our third summer in Bucolia, always a bit slow on the uptake, I had learned a valuable trick. From then on, whenever I felt enslaved by the barbeque and in danger of going without food, let alone rubbing elbows with our guests while they (and I) were still relatively sober, I would corral anyone who chanced to stop and express even a passing interest in grilling, asking them with a big, friendly, bucolic smile, "Say, would you mind watching this for me for a minute? I have to go check on something." Before you could say "Wabash Cannonball," I would bequeath tong and spatula to the unsuspecting sap and make myself scarce as a Buffalo nickel, piling a plate high with a Dr. Seuss-style mountain of burgers, with *two* bottles of Merlot under my arm.

But soiree season doesn't shift into high gear until we're all set to celebrate our nation's birthday. Donna and I have decided to simplify this particular soiree, gastronomically speaking, since things are likely to become, shall we say, downright animated as Independence Day rolls on. So, we supply the fundamental main course, consisting of a burger bar. Which means I grill a whole mess of burgers in a short period of time, while a table full of buns and condiments is laid out, forming an assembly line of delights. The guests? They can bring whatever their stomachs desire, just as long as it has nothing to do with burgers. Seems to work quite nicely.

What makes the Fourth of July unique in Bucolia is that, far from the interference of niggling neighbors or curious lawmen (who are greatly preoccupied elsewhere on the Fourth), we can pretty much shoot off and blow up anything that strikes our fancy. And we pretty much do. Donna feels compelled to put me on a budget when it comes to the purchasing of pyrotechnics, so I have to seek out allies in the quest to produce the loudest and brightest of extravaganzas.

Since we had encountered a spot of bad luck on a prior Fourth of July (specifically the bovine Independence Day breakout you're about to encounter), and because the fields around our home tend to be a bit on the dry, combustible side by early July, our family and posse have happily accepted the gracious invitation from our neighbors across the road to join them and theirs down at the river for the Fourth. It's a perfect solution: two barbeques followed by one big bucolic blast.

Afterward, with full bellies, singed fingertips, empty bottles, and full cups, the glowingly patriotic gathering is likely to burst into song. What is it with music and bucolic soirees? Hard to say. There's just something harmonic and melodic to living in general out here. That something may not always translate well into our vocal cords, but we do feel obliged to at least attempt to express that natural accord. So, late on the Fourth of July—it might well be the Fifth by then—you just might hear strains of "Yankee Doodle," "America the Beautiful," or "The Star Spangled Banner" wafting down the river and through the valley. The lyrics might be a bit muddled, but by God the spirit is there.

After Labor Day, which is always a bit tricky for party planners both inside Bucolia and outside in the allegedly real world on account of the mad dash of last-minute vacationers and the proximity of the first day of school, the opportunities for grand soirees start to thin out. Until Halloween, that is.

Probably because most all the chores and rewards of agrarian growing season have been completed and harvested, the end of October is prime time for celebration. So folks out here take their Halloweens seriously. There'll be costume parties galore, complete with homegrown bands and lots of dancin'. And there's likely to be a haunted house somewhere close by—a really ghoulish one that some devilish Bucolian put a lot of thought, fright, and hard-earned money into. Why? Maybe it was a good year for their berry fields. Maybe the price of milk or beef went up. Or maybe that daily commute into the

Big City finally paid off with a promotion. Who knows? But who can resist the temptation to invite the neighbors over for a simple costume party and then scare the holy Hell out of them?

Not long ago, one of our recent arrivals decided to introduce themselves to their new neighbors by throwing an open house party. A haunted open house party. Each and every room of their home, hallways included, was done up in a different terrifying theme. Zombies in one room, ghosts in another, crazy creepy babies in a third. On and on the ghastly tour proceeded, until I reached the one room I hoped they had neglected to include. But no. I turned a corner, and there they were.

Clowns leaning against a wall; clowns lying on a bed; clowns clawing their way out from under the bed; clowns hanging from the ceiling. All statues and stuffed figures, of course, and some rigged to turn their heads, smile menacingly or laugh insanely. Being a closet clownophobe who loathes anything to do with the infuriatingly inane creatures, I was just beginning to turn on my heel and beat a hasty retreat when something popped up at my elbow, looked me crazily in the eye and grinned, "Happy Halloween!" It was a real clown who had been sitting stiffly in a chair looking for all the world like one of his lifeless compatriots. I damn near punched the dude. Instead, scared poopless, I barked out a strangled nervous laugh, tripped over my own feet, and staggered, arms wildly outstretched, like a drunken mummy out of that accursed room. I'm not sure that I trust those neighbors to this day.

By the holiday season, I was almost fully recovered. Good thing, too, because like most places in the known world, there are parties aplenty from November to January here in Bucolia. Potlucks galore, as you might imagine, that feature all sorts of locally grown fare and home baked treats. I'm pretty sure I even spied figgy pudding once. Which is odd, because figs don't grow around here. Though I wouldn't be surprised to find that some enterprising Bucolian had discovered a way to do it. And, of course, following the hot homegrown apple pie topped with ice cream from the dairy across the valley, choruses of "Joy to the World," "Light One Candle," and "Auld Lang Syne" are apt to be heard echoing from house to house.

In Bucolia, we celebrate life. And sometimes it seems we live to celebrate.

The Great Independence Day Bovine Breakout

And when it comes to celebrating, our bovine neighbors don't want to be left out. Or, apparently, in.

It began as the perfect Third of July celebration here in Bucolia: lots of friends and neighbors joining Donna and I here on the hillside for barbequed burgers (both meaty and veggie), great conversation, political debate, fireworks, and song. True, as the Merlot flowed like, well, wine, the conversation waxed bawdy, the debate waned from finger-wagging to sloppy hugs, and errant bottle rockets increasingly threatened life and limb. But the off-key, lyrically challenged chorus around the fire warmed the hearts of one and all in grand anticipation of the following day's parades and additional public displays of pyrotechnics honoring the birth of our nation.

Little did we suspect as the glorious evening of the Third wound down to the wee hours of the Fourth that this particular Independence Day would bring panic, terror, and unholy chaos in the form of a dastardly sneak attack reminiscent of Pearl Harbor or the Trojan Horse.

But this was neither an airborne nor equine ambush. This was a sneak attack of the bovine kind.

After the rockets had ceased their red glaring, the choral cacophony ceased echoing through the valley, and most revelers had returned home while a brave few remained camped out in our back yard, all appeared right with the world. Donna and I toddled off to Slumbertown in expectation of a well-earned and lengthy night's sleep without disturbance until nigh upon noon of Fourth of July.

But my father-in-law's cattle had other ideas that fateful night. Ideas of flight and freedom.

True enough, we humans had encroached slightly upon their pasture just outside our yard in order to secure a somewhat safe launching pad for our various multicolored missiles. We propped a gate open as we dashed madly to and fro with our lighters and fuse-equipped instruments of mayhem. But the cows didn't seem to mind. In fact, they gathered at a prime viewing spot in a corner of the field, gazing in awe at the brightly erupting explosions in the sky, mooh-ing and maah-ing with bedazzled glee every bit as much as we humans ooh-ed and aah-ed.

Turns out it was all an act. All an extremely successful attempt to lull us two-legged spectators into a sense of serene security, as if we could be communing with our bovine counterparts in some sort of inter-species patriotic ecstasy. In retrospect, these Herefords were more likely plotting than spectating; more likely keeping an eye on us than watching the wondrous display.

For Donna and I were in for a rude awakening on that dreadful Fourth of July. Literally.

I'm not sure which came first: the shouting, the door-knocking, or the phone-ringing. Regardless, shortly after dawn, all hell broke loose. Bleary-eyed and fuzzy-headed, Donna and I were indeed rudely awakened to the sights and sounds of late-night campers milling around dazedly in our front yard and neighbors loudly inquiring about the status of our fence as our good friend across the road stared out over her morning cup of coffee and asked Donna over the phone, "This just doesn't look right to me; are there supposed to be cows in your garden?"

That didn't seem right to us, either. Generally, one keeps one's livestock in something called a pasture. Livestock in a yard or garden? Not highly recommended.

Yet sure enough, as we gazed dazedly out through our dining room windows into the hazy dawn of that Independence Day morning light, our bleary eyes gradually focused in on a bizarre, horrifying scene. Vernon's cattle were casually wandering our garden paths like so many fascinated yet hefty horticultural tourists. This was neither thistle nor grass, they no doubt puzzled, not clover or grain. The cows were in bovine heaven, sniffing and snorting this way and that, sampling roses, dahlias, dogwoods, berries, and begonias.

Slowly, a look of terror crept over Donna's face. What were these beasts doing in her carefully nurtured garden? Then terror gave way to anger. One misstep and any number of her floral children would be crushed to death!

Quietly, we cautiously opened our front door. The cows looked up, spied our presence, and began ambling out of the garden paths toward our driveway, figuring the garden tour must be at an end. Then it dawned on them: humans! Must run! Not supposed to be here, must escape! And down the driveway they bolted, straight across the road to our neighbor's path which led into the woods down by the river.

Vernon, by now alerted by his sixth cow sense, was ambling down the road when the stampede rushed past him. Even from the distance of our front porch, we could tell he was a tad upset. Might have been the unintelligible tirade he unleashed or the searing look he shot our way. It was clear he was reevaluating our desirability as neighbors. Or family.

By now, party guests, neighbors, and bemused onlookers had gathered in our driveway wondering what to do next. Clearly, the cattle had formulated a plan. They were long gone. It was decided to send a search party down to the river. Most likely, the cows were enjoying the cool shade of the woods or picnicking down at the beach. Middle of July in Bucolia? Why not?

Either they had solved the mystery of lifting gate latches or some traitorous July 3rd reveler had assisted in their escape. Whatever the case suffice it to say that, ecstatic to find themselves on the opposite side of the pasture fence, those Herefords were celebrating their Independence Day with great glee.

And so a cadre of friends, neighbors, and curious cow-hunters, spearheaded by Vernon, trouped down to the river, following winding woodland trails in search of telltale hoof prints and freshly laid cow poop.

Meanwhile, Donna, the legendary cow whisperer from the Battle of the Hillside, grabbed her keys, hopped into her Kia, and started heading up the road. Utterly befuddled and hovering undecidedly between the road and the river path, I asked Donna, "Where the hell are you going?"

"Just following a hunch," she calmly replied and idled slowly up the road.

Completely clueless and feeling downright helpless, I began to trudge uncertainly down toward the river-bound search party. Turns out the platoon of bovine trackers had fanned out: some scoured the woods; others scoured the riverbank, while our neighbor Denis took point, jogging along the edge of his own pasture in a courageous effort to cut off the cattle's line of retreat.

"Hello!" I shouted into the woods. "Any luck?"

"We're darn sure they're down here," bellowed Vernon in menacing tones. "We'll get 'em, all right!"

About seventeen seconds later, I spied a familiar blue Kia heading back down the road toward our house. I staggered up the river path to meet Donna as she leaned out the car window to report, "Mike up the road swears he saw the cows go up the creek behind his place. I'll go check it out." Donna smiled, hung a U-turn, and headed back up thataway.

Now fully flummoxed, I tromped back down toward the river and shouted into the woods like a mad sentinel, "Donna says the cows are way up the road by the creek next to Mike's place!"

"What?" Vernon shouted back. "Where?"

"Just come on out of there and up to the road! That's where they're supposed to be!"

Gradually, one by one, the scouting party straggled out of the woods, puzzled, tired, and ornery.

And as we all regrouped on the road, we gazed toward Mike's place, way up by the creek, to behold a truly mystifying sight. Rolling slowly down the road toward our house was a bizarre parade: a little blue car flanked by a whole bunch of cows.

Donna the cow whisperer led the cattle serenely back to our driveway where all we had to do was get them through the back yard gate into the pasture. But what followed next was not so serene. For one thing, once those cows recognized that they were back in our front yard, they suspected some evil plot was afoot to put a quick end to their Independence Day freedom. For another, we humans had forgotten how small the back yard gate was that we had to funnel the beasts through in order to return them to their rightful pasture.

So there we were: cows in the front yard garden, hemmed in by humans; our house between that potential battlefield and the back yard with the tiny gate; and Donna looking on with dawning horror as she began to realize the potential havoc to be wreaked upon her precious bushes and plants.

No one knows who made the first fateful move—just as no one knew how the doggone cows had escaped in the first place—but suddenly our garden turned into a frenzy of combat. Cows were snorting, reeling and tromping, humans were hooting, hollering, and herding. And Donna, poor cow-whispering Donna looked about ready to pass out.

Most of the cattle, figuring their human pursuers to be plum loco, after a bit of confused wheeling around, made haste for the back yard and the safety of their beloved pasture, barging their way by twos through the tiny gate. But one crazed fellow—there's always one, isn't there—insisted on circling the house, playing some insane bovine version of hide-n-seek, until at last he became entangled in a wire trellis that was supposed to have been home to a crop of Marionberries that never appeared. Whereupon he thought better of his childish shenanigans and headed for the gate as well.

All of us heaved a humongous sigh of relief as Vernon latched the gate, glaring at me with a withering look he no doubt reserved for the lowliest coyote, field snake, or barn rat. I simply hung my head and shambled back to the front yard to survey the horrific battleground that was once Donna's garden.

But lo! Incredibly, the verdant territory remained mostly intact. True, there was a broken branch here, a trampled plant there. And, of course, a bent and broken tangle of wire where the berry patch was intended to be. But, other than that, 98.7% of our plant friends, 100% of our human friends, and every one of Vernon's beloved bovines had survived the Great Independence Day Breakout.

I made a mental note to find a new venue for next year's 3rd of July celebration, Donna made a mental note to keep a closer eye on me and my friends, and Vernon made a mental to note to find himself a new son-in-law.

As for the cows? Oh, the bright, sparkling lights against the night sky; oh, the wonderful garden tour; oh the unforgettable memories of freedom!

Chapter 13: Blessed are the Zone Fives, for They Shall Inherit the Pasture

Time was, when Donna and I first started converting pastureland into garden, that we'd take a moment to offer a prayer and a blessing for each new plant we laid ever so gently into the ground. Now, we just buy perennials by the dozens, dig like mad, add a little compost and water, hope the plants have a prayer of surviving our Bucolian winters, and feel blessed if they do somehow manage to resuscitate themselves come April or May.

Yes, it seems like many moons ago when first we thrust spade into turf, laboriously turning over patch after patch of sod, only to reveal the sand and endless rocks beneath. Oh, how many bags of fertilizer we lugged, how many yards of soil we shoveled from truck to ragged weed patch. Not to mention agonizing over the choice and position of each new addition to our nascent garden. It was like meticulously planning a family—how many of this type of plant, how many of that; exact measurements of the proper spacing; should we put this short one in the shade of that tall one; what time of year were they likely bloom, and what color would those blossoms be?

Naturally, just as though we were raising a family, Donna and I earnestly attempted to invoke the assistance of a Higher Power. Being lovers of nature and of life itself, we weren't exactly honed in on Who or What that Higher Power might be, so we leaned heavily on Native American traditions gleaned from close friends who themselves were learned in ancient indigenous wisdom and were closely allied with and knowledgeable of the plant kingdom.

Hence, for our first two springs in Bucolia, we treated each new addition to our garden with a blessing of tobacco (this necessitated frequent trips to convenience stores for pouches of Drum and Top, even though Donna never smoked and I had quit over 20 years ago), a plant-by-plant personalized "thank you for joining us," and general "welcome to the garden." No doubt this piqued the interest of our neighbors, who, wandering down the road, probably raised an eyebrow or two watching me lean over each freshly planted flower, shrub or tree while mumbling an apparent incantation and tossing shreds of something-or-other onto root and leaf.

It was indeed my duty to actually formulate and intone the words of welcome. Why? Well, I was the "creative one" of our team (i.e. the conjurer of imaginative ideas that folks absolutely adored but resulted in very little fiscal reward), and the "spiritual one" as well (having attended seminary at Yale Divinity School decades ago, resulting in similarly paltry financial return). Clearly, I was perfectly suited for the job of blessing plants; it was the least I could do. Literally.

For instance, when it came time to install three new Yarrow starts in various plots around the garden, I would draw upon my fond memories of the folk singers Peter, Paul, and Mary, cleverly recalling that Peter's last name was Yarrow. "Welcome, Yarrow," I would enthuse while bending over the seedling, "thank you so much for adding your color and song to our home! May you blow happily in the wind for many years to come, along with your cousins Paul (a Lemon Yarrow) and Mary (a Yarrow nicknamed "Saucy Seduction"). Welcome to our family!" And I'd sprinkle some tobacco on the unsuspecting groundcover, whilst taking a sip or three from the Sacred Cup of Amber. Which, by the way, would be Scotch and soda. Let's face it, every ceremonial celebrant is entitled to partake of the Holy Libation of his choice (as revealed to him by the Book of the *Drunken Botanist*) in order to enhance the effect of the event.

But I wouldn't always stop with a blessing, a thank you, a welcome. I'd ask that the taller shrubs shade and protect the smaller plants. I'd ask that the trees provide shelter for our winged visitors. I'd ask the Yarrow's groundcover buddies to spread and prosper, securing the soil for their friends around them. Sometimes I'd request that the newbies multi-task: bring color, attract bees, lure hummingbirds, resist deer, store raindrops, endure drought, dance in the sunlight, sing at night. It all depended on how many Sacred Cups of Amber I had imbibed.

So now you have the neighbors staring in awe as this insane newcomer staggers from flower to flower, drink sloshing crazily in one hand ("watering" every inch of soil and stone along the way, giving new meaning to "Scotch on the Rocks"), a rumpled pouch of god-knows-what clutched in the other, while, yes, mumbling an apparent incantation and tossing shreds of something-or-other onto root and leaf. Come to think of it, it did take a while for our fellow dwellers on our lonely road to approach and get to know us. I always wondered why, given that we were such ardent gardeners and fellow lovers of the land. Just one of life's great mysteries, I guess.

Nonetheless, we soldiered on with the planting and the blessing. But by the spring of our third year in Bucolia, a great truth had been revealed to us: frost kills. Or, to be precise: repeated frosts kill. When you live on a hillside in a valley in the shadow of a mountain, spring comes in fits and starts. One sunny morning in February, you'll awaken from winter's chill to discover that it's 45 degrees outside. Oh joy, an early spring! It'll stay sunny and warm for a few days, as sleepy plants pop their heads warily out of the soil, and you'll begin planning trips to the local nurseries, sifting through seed packets, sketching out plans for the next section to be planted. Just when you're ready to don your gloves and rummage around in the shed for your shovel and hoe, a fresh freeze will suddenly seize the land. The curious plants retreat, the ground hardens, and winter reclaims its deathly hold.

In Bucolia, this horrific process repeats itself not just once or twice, but several times over the passage of many weeks: heat, frost, heat, frost, heat, frost. Until finally, worn down by winter's endless siege, many plants have just plain surrendered and given up the futile attempt to burst forth and bloom only to wither in the face on an unexpected freeze. By mid-March, the typical Bucolian garden is a ghastly wasteland of brown blossoms and withered stems, a botanical Antietam of heroic flora sacrificed in the harrowing march from winter to spring.

Faced with such insurmountable odds, we gradually gave up the high-minded notion of blessing and welcoming each and every plant to our hillside. Instead, we adopted a tactic of throwing increasing numbers of botanic soldiers into the breach in an attempt to overwhelm the forces of the Frost King, praying quickly with mass blessings of the green horde, "*Good Lord*, we hope *some* of you survive until next April!"

The upshot being, nowadays when we search for plants, exotic blossoms and variegated foliage don't hold the fascination they used to. The first thing we look for now is, how hardy is this puppy? If it's a Zone 5 or lower, blessed be, it might just survive our hillside battleground. This despite the fact that the United States Department of Agriculture insists that we dwell in Zone 8. Hah! I dare you to send us your Zone 8 wimps and dandies, USDA. Guaranteed they'll suffer the fate of poets and priests faced by the icy swords of the unforgiving Phalanx o' Jack the Frost! No lover of the weak are Jack and his minions.

Still, a lover of the roses am I. Still, Jack usually gets the best of me and my beloveds. Strange thing, though: I have discovered over the years that, regardless of the alleged hardiness of any particular rose, be it tea, floribunda, or climber, the more money I spend on a rose, the less likely it is to survive. I'll shell out megabucks for a rose that bursts forth with gloriously gigantic and fabulously fragrant peach blossoms only to find that it, like a brilliant bottle rocket, will gloriously burst, fade and pass never to return again. On the other hand, those sickly end-of-season stragglers that I've bought on close-out for $4.99, those gangly stringers donated by well-meaning friends, have tended to last year after year, producing blooms as numerous and verdant as the weeds at their feet.

We've had somewhat better luck when it comes to edible flora. Or fruita. Or vegeta. Whatever. Our most glaring failures there manifest themselves—or, more correctly, fail to manifest themselves—in the fruita category.

There's a well-regarded nursery close by that pretty much dedicates itself to the cultivation of fruit trees and berry bushes. They boast row upon row of apple trees, cherry trees, plum trees, peach trees, pear trees, hazel nut trees, beezlenut trees, nectarcadorino trees. And berries? Strawberries, raspberries, blueberries, gooseberries, dingleberries, bucoliberries. You name it, they have it. They don't have it, they'll graft it. Want to cross a kiwi with a cherry, a huckleberry with a grape? Consider it done. Next summer you'll be swimming in cherrykees and grapleberries.

But of the seven fruit trees we corralled from this esteemed bastion of horticulture, only two remained after the first winter. So now our garden is winsomely graced with one Charlie-Brown-style scraggly-assed apple tree (complete with one apple that never seems to ripen) and one pie cherry tree that's bursting with the sourest cherries known to man. We've tried to entice our neighbors, "Come, help yourselves to our abundant crop of cherries. Perfect for a pie, or twelve!" No takers. They'd rather buy their pie at the bakery in town, thank you very much. And the family of deer that dwells in our woods? Oh, they do appreciate the dogwoods and roses we so kindly grow for their gastronomic pleasure. But even they won't touch our bounteous if dolefully sour cherries.

And then there's the mysterious plum tree. It managed to last two seasons, even filled up with blossoms the second. But the third?

Dead as a doornail. Trunk split. But the birds seemed to like its bare branches, so I hung a few little wind chimes and decorations on the poor dude, an impromptu ode to Springmas in Bucolia, and the birds and I had a grand old time with the ex-plum. Then something green began appearing from its trunk. It grew and grew and grew some more. Continues to grow to this very day. What is it? No one seems to know. But it's a bit scary. What kind of alien flora sprouts and thrives from a dead tree? Even the birds are keeping their distance. I wouldn't be at all surprised if the wind chimes and other baubles began disappearing. I'm keeping my eye on this zombie plum. One false move, and it's hacksaw time.

Speaking of scary, I wonder if the producers of some of those old B-movie sci-fi flicks weren't berry growers. You know how they used to come up with those macabre beasts complete with slithering tentacles? Well, Donna and I quickly discovered that if you let your raspberry vines (sorry, I meant *canes*—mustn't anger the agricultural police here in Bucolia) go long enough without a tie-up or trim, pretty soon you'll have Razilla threatening your garden. Tentacles everywhere, greedily reaching for the nearest unsuspecting plant, bush, or human foot. Oh sure, if you carefully tend the canes, then you'll be the recipient of luscious fruit for years to come. But turn your back on them and the Dark Side will emerge. Then you're more likely to find yourself tripped up and falling flat on your face in a bed of zucchini than enjoying a delicious dollop of raspberry jam.

Zucchini: now there's a plant even I can grow. Just plop a few seeds in the ground and in a month or two you'll have 87 gourds the size of the Hindenburg. But beware: just like pie cherries, zucchini are virtually impossible to give away. Because, for some reason, no one seems to remember from one year to the next how splendidly zucchini reproduce. So, every summer and fall here in Bucolia, baskets and boxes of zucchini will appear without warning on front doorsteps, the seats of unlocked parked cars, in mailboxes, leashed to unattended pets, perched atop fence posts, in the arms of unsuspecting children—anything is fair game when it comes to disposing of excess zucchini.

Admittedly, Donna and I may have waxed a bit over-ambitious when embarking on our first sewing of vegetables in our new garden. Well, it wasn't much of a garden back then. More like a sparsely tilled former pasture whose only proven produce at the time was rocks. Rocks of all sizes, rocks of all shapes. Every dip of a spade into the soil brought forth a fresh harvest of rocks. Nonetheless, newly arrived from the confines of garden-less city living, we went hog-wild.

We decided to begin with tomatoes. Easy enough, right? Heck, you can grow your own tomatoes on a porch or in a windowsill, or so I've heard. So off to the local organic nursery we went, humming merry gardening tunes along the way.

What we encountered there blew our urbanite minds. Row upon row of small green starts adorned long tables that stretched far into the distance. Who knew there were so many kinds of tomatoes? Beefsteak, Cherokee Purple, Early Girl, Mortgage Lifter, Roma, Super Sweet 100, Sweet Million, Yellow Pear…on and on the list went. I had assumed we'd simply be choosing between the little ones (cherry tomatoes) or the big ones (well, *big* tomatoes—I'm so confused by now, I'm not sure what to call them). So we just sort of casually browsed the endless rows, reading the descriptions and looking at the photos on the stakes. Every now and then, we'd pick up a plant, mumble something like, "Ooh, this looks interesting," and place it in our cart.

Following similar journeys of discovery regarding the various and sundry types of *Solanum lycopersicum*, we wound up bringing home 13 varieties of tomatoes in all. Ought to be enough to feed two people, right? And maybe leave a little left over for canning?

So we returned home with our green-leafed treasures, scraped 13 spots bare of the scrubbly grass and weeds, gouged 13 holes into the rock-infested crust, planted our babies, and awaited the abundant harvest to come. But their growth seemed stunted. Might have had something to do with the Martian-like clayish desert into which they'd been so ingloriously introduced. So off to the feed store I went in search of straw (not hay—yes, there is a difference; no, I still haven't figured it out). We caressed our infant tomato plants with said straw and watered them so mightily that even Mars would have brought forth a tomato or two just in order to make the deluge desist.

A few plants struggled bravely out of the sodden muck, and it began to look as though our diligent efforts would be rewarded with a bumper crop. But then autumn came. It began to rain. It kept raining, then rained some more. Our remaining band of hardy stragglers began to take on a decidedly droopy appearance, then became downright sickly.

It was then that we became acquainted with the agricultural term "tomato blight." Ugly dark spots had magically appeared, covering virtually our entire crop. A desperate search for survivors revealed exactly three nicely formed, ripe, unscathed tomatoes remaining out of the whole herd of 13 promising plants.

But those were the three tastiest tomatoes Donna and I had ever eaten. Somewhere, Martians were staring down on us with far-away wonder, licking their Martian lips.

That's when we decided to lay in a supply of boards, brackets, professional grade weed cloth, and imported enriched soil. The era of raised garden beds loomed on the horizon.

But perhaps the most amazing aspect of growing your own vegetables is that, when at last you get to sample the results, it's as though you've created a time machine for your taste buds. Two things happened when I bit into my first home-grown tomato: 1) I wished I'd worn a bib, because juice squirted everywhere, splashing my glasses and running down my chin, and 2) I was immediately transported back in time to when I was about six years old, eating tomatoes our family routinely bought from the local farm stand. With one sudden jarring jolt, I remembered what tomatoes are supposed to taste like! These weren't hothouse supermarket "tomatoes" that simply tasted like, well, something red and a little watery. These were luscious, juicy, delicious tomatoes that simply seethed with flavor and just plain healthy goodness.

I dashed to the lettuce, yanked off a leaf, munched it. I remember this, too! It's the crisp, tasty stuff that Mom used to put under the tomatoes in her salads! I grabbed a cucumber, twisted it free from its vine, bit a chunk out of the middle. My grandmother's cucumber sandwiches! I yanked up a radish. I used to steal these off my dad's plate when he wasn't looking (he was, and smiling, too)…what *are* those bland, round, red marbles they sell in stores? And so I zipped from plant to plant like a hummingbird among foxgloves or a kid (which I felt like and no doubt closely resembled) among the gifts on Christmas morning.

Nothing was the same, everything old but new again. All of Bucolia is truly a time machine: whether it stems from a well-cared-for garden or arises from a casual conversation over a fence post: everything old but new again.

Chapter 14: Radio Bucolia

Part I: Radiophile

"We interrupt our regularly scheduled programming *for this special bulletin..."* - Newscasters preparing you to hear something momentous, usually really bad.

"I'm fed up to the ears with old men dreaming up wars for young men to die in." – George McGovern.

"I'm so mean I make medicine sick." – Muhammad Ali.

"Swung on and missed, strike three. Looks like (Phillies, Giants, Angels, Mariners, fill in the blank) fans will have to wait till next year." – Any sportscaster of any baseball team I've ever followed.

"And now it's time for the Top Ten countdown!" – AM DJs all over America.

Just some of the words I have heard over the years that made me fall in love with radio. Two exact quotes, and the other three—well, you get the gist.

I can hardly remember *not* listening to radio, and many of my most vivid memories consist of words spoken by someone at the other end of a box or dashboard dial rather than from images on a screen. But then I've always been more partial to words than pictures. Which likely explains why I fancy myself a writer as opposed to an artist.

I just don't understand visual art. Oh sure, I guess I can appreciate a beautifully rendered landscape, portrait, or still-life as well as the next person. As long as the next person is severely challenged when it comes to drawing even the most rudimentary stick figure. That's me. I seem to be fundamentally unable to visualize anything, much less translate that image into a sensible depiction. God forbid I should ever be called to the witness stand as an eyewitness to a crime.

Attorney: Mr. Thuney, how would you describe the assailant?

Me: Oh…about average height, average build.

Attorney: And hair color?

Me: Brown, I think.

Attorney: Brown, you think?

Me: Or possibly bald. Maybe wearing a hat?

Attorney: And how would you say the assailant was dressed?

Me: Casually. Maybe earth tones.

Attorney: So…perhaps a work shirt and khaki pants?

Me: Either that or a three-piece suit.

Attorney (gesturing toward the defendant): Mr. Thuney, do you see the assailant in the courtroom here today?

Me: Wait…did I say it was a guy? Might have been a mannish-looking woman. Carrying a floral handbag.

Judge (with a long sigh): I knew I should have retired last year and run for Congress.

Me: Hang on; I *do* see that bastard in the courtroom! Third row, fifth seat from the left. No, wait, that's my chiropractor. He does a great job on my spine. I love it when he twists my neck just so…

Attorney: I object!

Judge: At this point, I think we all do. The witness is dismissed.

So it is. Images don't stick with me. Words do. Especially spoken words. Which is why I've had a love affair with radio since forever.

One November day in sixth grade, a classmate and I were called to the nurse's office for some reason or other. Hearing tests, as I recall. They must not do those anymore in school. Because it sure seems like kids can't hear a single thing adults say these days. But maybe that's always been the case, come to think of it. It is nice, though, that "selective hearing" is one of the few perks that we old farts get to fall back on as we, shall we say, mature. If we don't want to respond to or act on whatever's being discussed, we just pretend we didn't hear it. Same thing with memory. Don't want to do something? Sorry, it just slipped my mind! It's all a very well guarded secret, and I hope I haven't let the cat out of the bag. But what the heck was that cat doing in the bag in the first place? I can't seem to remember.

So, there we were in the nurse's office, just happy to be dodging class for a little while. While the nurse checked us in, shuffling through a file, a radio on her desk droned quietly in the background. Then a voice came on the radio, an insistent voice. The nurse looked up in alarm and suddenly dropped her papers. My classmate and I glanced at each other: had we done something wrong? Were we both about to be told that we were going deaf due to some bizarre disease? Then we saw the nurse's eyes start to fill with tears, as she fearfully turned up the volume on the radio. A newscaster, barely able to contain his own emotions, was desperately trying to describe a horrific scene in a faraway place called Dallas, Texas. We heard something about a woman in a car jumping up out of her seat, shouting, "Oh, no!" Then she scrambled onto the back of the car crying for help.

The nurse cleared her throat, tried her best to gather her wits, and motioned for a woman in an adjoining office to come over.

"We had better get these children back to their classroom," said the nurse, "President Kennedy's been shot."

And so it was that we were the first kids at Red Hill Elementary School to learn of the assassination of John F. Kennedy. Our teacher, curious to know why we had returned to the class so soon, asked if anything was the matter. "The president's been shot," we said, not really quite knowing what that meant yet. The teacher's face turned pale, then he began shaking his head as if to say, these children are pulling some cruel prank, this cannot be real. But it was real. We had heard it on the radio. And, seconds later, our teacher was hearing it from the principal who contacted every classroom to inform every teacher that President Kennedy had been gravely wounded.

No, I couldn't conceive of what it all meant right then. But many folks feel that the American Dream died that day, and, in retrospect, I cannot argue with that. The essentially American traits of compassion, cooperation, optimism, and adventure began slowly to fade away after November 22, 1963, and precious little has been seen of them since.

Not every radio memory was quite that traumatic, though. Having been raised by my dad to be a boxing fan, as a teenager I quickly latched onto the skyrocketing career of an audacious young Olympic hero named Cassius Clay. Most of America seemed to like him back then, even grudgingly putting up with his brash attitude and silly rhymes. But when Cassius Clay adopted Islam and became Muhammad Ali? Well, that was a horse of a different color. Almost literally. While many of my fellow pinkskins disowned him after that, I found Ali and his newfound faith fascinating. I even wrote up a research paper about Islam for a high school project. And I delighted as Muhammad Ali devastated each and every heavyweight contender in his path. Conversely, my heart sank when he was bested by Joe Frazier following a lengthy layoff due to Ali's controversial stand against the Vietnam War draft.

Then along came an ostensibly mean-spirited menace of a man named George Foreman. Foreman seemed to knock out everyone he faced in record time. He glared, he glowered, his fists were deadly weapons. He even made quick work of the presumably unbeatable Joe Frazier. I can still hear legendary announcer Howard

Cosell's shocked voice shouting, "Down goes Frazier! Down goes Frazier!"

So when Ali enthusiastically agreed to fight Foreman for the title, I was deeply chagrined. This will be the end of my hero, I thought. No one can possibly survive the savage whirlwind that is George Foreman.

There was no network TV coverage of the fight, which took place in a distant land known as Zaire. You had to wait—ever so patiently— for round-by-round summaries to emerge from the local radio affiliate. As each round passed by, the summaries seemed the same: Ali was taking a horrible beating, pinned against the ropes by Foreman's constant barrage of heavy blows. It gradually became apparent that my worst fears were being realized. Ali would be lucky to survive this fight, and even the announcer seemed to grow weary of narrating the vicious pummeling from one round to the next. The summaries began to lag behind, probably due to the assumption that even the most ardent listener would have shut off the radio by now.

Still, I clung to my portable radio, hanging grimly onto every last word, every last hope. When the summary of the eighth round came much sooner than expected, I myself began reaching for the OFF switch. But the stunned announcer recounted with complete disbelief that the apparently worn-out Ali had come off the ropes and knocked George Foreman down and out. I felt like my sixth-grade teacher upon hearing of JFK's assassination: this isn't possible; it's someone's idea of a clever hoax or cruel joke. But it was real. And, again, I had heard it on the radio. That's one of the last times I can remember being ecstatic about the outcome of a boxing match.

Other peak-of-joy and valley-of-despair moments of elation and disappointment were to follow, emanating from the speaker of a radio. I vividly recall waiting up until the wee hours of the morning to hear another hero of mine give his historic acceptance speech. South Dakota Senator George McGovern had won the Democratic nomination following a bitter and protracted battle with Minnesota Senator Hubert H. Humphrey. I hung onto his every word, thinking, "This is the next President of the United States. Nobody in their right mind would want to re-elect Richard Nixon."

On election night, as I drove home with a carful of optimistic McGovern volunteers, weary from a day of doorbelling and ferrying voters to the polls, the car radio informed us of the disastrous results. Clearly, a whole lot of Americans were not in their right minds.

But before boxing, there was baseball. My affection for baseball stems from way back in my childhood. However, being a short, scrawny, sickly kid, I found following the game far more enjoyable than playing it. Two memories stand out from my brief and unheralded Little League career. The first was, whenever our team desperately needed a baserunner, the coach would call on good ol' Matt Thuney. Because I was a great hitter, blessed with lightning speed? Hardly. Being the shortest kid on the field, and also being coached into batting out of an extreme crouch, my strike zone was miniscule. I'd be sent up to the plate simply to take pitches and hope for a walk. Which resulted in my second vivid recollection.

Toward the end of the season, in yet another instance where the coach sent me up to the batter's box to coax a walk, I had finally had enough. I decided right then and there to take a mighty cut at the next good pitch I saw. I did. The ball cracked soundly off the bat and went soaring high in the air toward left field. With my mind screaming home run—or at least extra bases—I put my head down and started running for all I was worth. Which, sadly, wasn't much. I rounded first base just in time to look up and see the ball drop harmlessly into the shortstop's glove. He hadn't moved an inch. My tape-measure homer had turned into an infield pop-up. I lowered my head once again and headed for the dugout, picking out a seat on the beach as far away as possible from my scowling coach. Silently I thanked the baseball gods that no one was hearing a broadcast of that game.

On the heels of my inglorious retirement from Little League, I found it was far easier to root for a team than to play for one. I embraced our hometown teams with great gusto, catching every game I could on our home or car radio. Unfortunately, my chosen teams in those days, namely the Philadelphia Phillies and Los Angeles Angels, rarely played with great gusto. Listening to their helpless travails year after year proved to be every bit as disappointing as my attempt to play the game. But a little less painful and damaging to my budding psyche.

My single-minded devotion to those sportscasts did, however, help to hone my problem-solving skills. One year as a birthday present I received a state-of-the-art Japanese transistor radio complete with earplug attachment. Overjoyed, I proceeded to concoct a foolproof system whereby I could surreptitiously listen to October World Series games while pretending to pay attention during class at school. The World Series was primarily composed of day games back then—and needless to say, my favorite teams never saw the light of *those* days—but still I would adopt one of the unfamiliar combatants and live or die on every pitch. Thus was invented the patented Thuney Hidden Ballgame Trick. I would tuck the transistor radio into my pants pocket, poke a hole in the top of said pocket, and run the earplug cord up through the pants to my shirt into my sleeve and out the long-sleeved cuff, wedging the earplug into my ear which I then leaned on the palm of my hand, striking a pose of rapt attention as the teacher at the front of the classroom rambled earnestly on and on about textiles, long division, subject-verb agreement, or larvae and pupae. Frankly, I had no idea. But I did know what Mickey Mantle had done in his previous at-bat, and soon became the most popular kid at recess, as guys would gather around to hear my inning-by-inning updates.

So radio and I have always remained fast friends, and I forever envied the people behind the voices that kept me up-to-date on everything from the latest news to the sports scores to the weather report to the current top ten singles on the swingin' rock'n'roll charts.

I was ecstatic to finally hear the latest Beatles tune, would see how fast I could change the dial whenever cloying surf music came on (I still consider the Beach Boys and Jan and Dean to be threats to my aural health), and closely monitored the rise and fall of each and every "super-group" to come along. It was the Golden Age of Rock and a pretty darn good one for radio in general as well.

As adulthood and the workaday world barged their way rudely into my life, I still managed to cling to radio, though, tuning in whenever I could. Just as I eventually came to the realization that I probably wouldn't be playing second base for the Philadelphia Phillies anytime soon, I also figured the radio business was nowhere in my foreseeable future. I just didn't possess the gift of gab that most radio personalities did. Still, I could always listen.

Then events took a strange turn. Bucolia came a-callin'.

Part II: Low Power, High Hopes

After I relocated to the Pacific Northwest, for several years, I had been writing humor columns and feature articles for local and regional newspapers and magazines, in addition to owning and running my own business in a small yet comfortable city. One day, an editor approached me with the idea of running a story about an organizational meeting being held by some folks who were starting a local low-power FM station out in the styx. Of course I jumped at the chance, and just hoped I could find the place without getting too lost along the way.

Well, I did get lost along the way, but not in a directional sense. I lost myself in the sheer joy and possibility of bearing witness to the birth of a brand-spanking new radio station.

The subsequent article, which appeared in an April 2007 issue of a now-defunct but then wildly popular newsmagazine called *Whatcom Independent*, went like this:

KAVZ-FM

SMALL COMMUNITY, BIG VOICE

By Matthew Thuney

For the *Whatcom Independent*

"For me, it's been a lifelong dream," mused retired Motorola technician Marcus Burton. It was Sunday afternoon, March 25, at the Van Zandt Community Hall, and Burton had just completed his presentation about the do's, don'ts, and how-to's of producing a music show for radio broadcast. The following Sunday, April 1, KAVZ-FMLP 102.5 would switch on its transmitter and officially begin broadcasting.

What does this brand-spanking new community radio station's alphabet soup of FCC call letters stand for? You probably already know that any station's signal west of the Mississippi begins with a K rather than a W. Ditto that FM refers to the broader bandwidth of frequency modulation as opposed to the more directional amplitude modulation of AM radio. The LP stands for low power, as in KAVZ's signal will only reach out about ten miles. And the AVZ initials refer to the very roots of this community effort, that it's centered in the towns of Acme and Van Zandt in the Mount Baker Foothills.

The process that led to the birth of KAVZ has been neither quick nor cheap. Indeed, earlier this year it looked like the station might be stillborn for lack of funds.

Brian Allen, who has been involved in promoting and producing community radio since 1984, began the project after he met up with Holly O'Neil while visiting the River Farm collective (yes, that old "hippie commune" as some neighboring farmers still refer to it, out at the south end of Hillside Road in Van Zandt) a few years back. In 1999, the Clinton Administration had, much to the consternation of certain corporate media interests, passed legislation paving the way for low-power community radio. Allen and O'Neil sought to take advantage of this new opportunity by proposing just such a radio outlet along the Nooksack River in the Mount Baker Foothills.

In June of 2001, an application was filed with the Federal Communications Commission. The project languished for a while, until it became more and more clear that the priceless FCC license would expire unless KAVZ actually got on the air. A construction permit was acquired for the station's studio at the Van Zandt Community Hall in April 2004. That's when the "fun" began. A base had to be built for the antenna mast. Improvements to the Community Hall's septic system were suddenly required. As Brian Allen recalls, "the whole permit process was a crazy thing."

Then there was the problem of money. It may seem as though a radio station magically appears out of freewheeling ether of voices and music. But it takes big bucks and loads of equipment to generate and transmit those ethereal sounds. Such as: the aforementioned mast and antenna, an FM transmitter, a decoder and receivers, computer hardware and software, iPod technology, a gaggle of cable and connectors, phone line, and on and on.

How much does that add up to? Let's see…add, multiply, divide by pi, carry the six…roughly $8,000 worth of equipment. Not so much, you say? Well, to a valleyful of cattlemen and organic farmers, that's a lot of hay and herbs. Silicon Valley, this ain't.

As 2007 dawned and the expiration date of KAVZ's license application loomed, financial panic set in. Holly O'Neil, longtime River Farm resident and community organizer, quickly cobbled together a fundraising drive, reaching out to everyone she could touch in the Foothills, their friends and family from afar, and those with an abiding interest in community radio in general. A deadline of February 28 was set to raise a minimum of $5,000. The supporters of "South Fork Community Radio," as O'Neil calls it (as in, the South Fork of the Nooksack River) gathered in the Van Zandt Community Hall that evening, anxiously awaiting the results of their *networking efforts. Would KAVZ receive the actual dollars it needed to make the dream reality?*

As mail envelopes were opened, checks counted, and walk-in cash wandered through the door, the donations poured in. The money had come, the station was saved. Apparently, this was one lifelong dream/crazy thing whose time had come, septic tank and all.

While the physical parts of the low-power FM station were purchased and put together, a vision began to take shape regarding the content of its broadcasts. "I believe some core values of this station would be celebration and honor," commented O'Neil in a recent email message to supporters, "It's going to be a really cool thing."

The supporters of KAVZ would like everyone in the community to get into the act and onto the air. Longtime community radio booster Dennis Lane likens the licensing of local low-power radio to "a kind of Homestead Act of the airwaves," noting that after five years of successful broadcasting, such a station's license will actually belong to the entire community. "It's a way of giving communities a voice," observes Lane.

According to Dudley and Dean Evenson, proprietors of the Deming-based music production company Soundings of the Planet, KAVZ will begin with entirely pre-recorded, automated programming which will include music (much of it by local performers) ranging from bluegrass to alternative rock, political discussion, public affairs, news from the Nooksack Tribe, and some shows borrowed from fellow low-power FM station KMRE in Bellingham. That's the beginning, but much more is planned, such as an effort to involve Mount Baker High School. "We need to bring the kids in and get them involved," advises Dudley Evenson. A KAVZ website is also in the works. "Eventually," says Evenson, "we'll reach the whole world through the Internet."

Apart from the web presence, the physical broadcast (currently 100 watts) may soon increase as well. If KAVZ goes to full power in the future, it could reach well beyond the small communities of Acme, Van Zandt, Wickersham and Deming. So what begins life as a community's simple desire to have its voice heard may grow into a greater commitment with a broader expression. There's a lot at stake in this tiny effort, and Brian Allen is well aware of the overall implications. "Without independent media," asserts Allen, "we're going to lose our democracy."

So next time you're taking the scenic route through eastern Whatcom County, cruising south toward Skagit County on Highway 9, you might want to reach over to your car radio and scan to 102.5 FM. What'll you hear? Maybe some new local music, maybe some Native American voices, maybe an amusing or informative interview...or just maybe the heartbeat of a community you never heard from before.

As it turned out, that remarkable resuscitation was relatively short-lived. Although I personally continued to be drawn to that same bucolic hamlet (reporting on everything from the local landmark yet nationally known country market known as Everybody's Store, to a proposed mega-highway which would have carved up and ground down the entire valley in order to provide a commerce corridor for oil, gas, and greedy-eyed bankers), little was to be heard from KAVZ, the little community radio station that could. Or could it?

Part III: The Voice of the Valley

It wasn't until 2011, just three years after Donna and I had at last heeded the call of Bucolia and had our house dragged over a mountain, that I once again crossed paths—or waves, as it were—with the long-forgotten, somewhat forlorn, KAVZ.

One last attempt was made to bring the station back to life. A community meeting was held, and several ardent radiophiles like me sat in curious attendance. Potential volunteers were asked to stand up, tell a bit about themselves and their experience in radio (if any), and relate how they might be willing to help out with the station.

A few folks stood, said wonderful things about how they loved radio, how a community radio station could be so beneficial to the region, and what kind of programming they'd like to hear. They were a bit short on specifics as to how exactly they might be of assistance.

Finally, I stood, told how I had trained at the "world famous" (more likely infamous) Columbia School of Broadcasting in San Francisco back in the days of scratchy old vinyl records, learned a bit about copy writing and newscasting for radio, been a host and guest on a few shows since then, really didn't feel particularly qualified to be on-air, but would be happy to help. I sat back down, assuming someone else with genuine experience and qualifications would magically appear. No one did. The organizers at the front of the room looked at each other, then at me. I, apparently, was their "someone else."

And so the meetings continued, programming was scheduled (thankfully, thousands of songs were donated by locals—some in the music biz, others just plain aficionados), budgets set (very meager budgets), and the time came to create and record on-air announcements. No one felt particularly competent to script copy for station IDs, public service announcements, music block introductions and the like, much less confident enough to put their vocal chords over the air. KAVZ needed someone else with writing and announcing experience to do all that. You can probably guess who that someone else was. Again.

I went online, purchased an inexpensive but highly recommended plug-in microphone for my laptop, downloaded the latest free edition of Audacity recording software and spent two or three maddeningly frustrating weeks figuring out how it all worked.

Meanwhile, it was also decided that KAVZ needed a tagline. "Your Voice of the Valley" won unanimous approval. We also needed a news and events program. Hence, "Echoes of the Valley." Maybe someone else could come up with some entertaining programming? Someone else did. He offered up his observations on how he was adjusting to country living, recorded those silly, self-deprecating pieces, and put them on the air from time to time.

"Bucolia" had been born.

I was asked to record some station IDs: "You are listening to KAVZ-LP 102.5 FM, your Voice of the Valley," that sort of thing. Naturally, I was incapable of simply providing straightforward announcements. I found it necessary to put my own creative (i.e. weird) twist on these fundamental requirements of broadcasting. So here's what our listening audience was forced to suffer through:

- My Ronald Reagan impersonation: "There you go again, listening to KAVZ-LP FM 102.5, Deming. A shining radio beacon down in the valley." It sounded more like W.C. Fields. With a bad hangover.
- "Ask not what KAVZ-LP FM 102.5, Deming, can do for you. Ask what you can do for KAVZ: Volunteer, donate, listen." JFK, of course. Or was it JFK impersonating FDR? Hard to tell.
- "Dude, do you hear that? It's KAVZ-LP FM 102.5 Deming. Whoa!" Jeff Spicoli from Fast Times at Ridgemont High. That's one I could easily have recorded 40 years ago. In my own voice. On any given Saturday night.
- "We have nothing to fear but KAVZ-LP FM 102.5. Nevertheless, we shall persevere! Cheers!" Okay, honestly, I thought this was a line Winston Churchill uttered amidst the woeful wreckage of World War II. Turns out it was FDR who delivered the famous line during the dark days of the Great Depression. Regardless, with my twisted and garbled interpretation, it might just as well have been Queen

Elizabeth. Or possibly Kermit the Frog's British cousin Dermot.

It's a wonder the Federal Communications Commission hasn't shown up with a briefcase full of summonses, reprimands, questionnaires, inquiries, injunctions, and indignation in general.

By the time the radio station was fully operational and had been broadcasting a steady stream of music and local programming on a regular basis, a massive event was scheduled to take place. And by massive event, I mean a Fourth of July parade a few miles down the highway that usually featured kids, dogs, a few costumes, and the occasional decked-out pickup truck. Our signal did reach that far, barely, but I couldn't imagine anyone had actually been listening. Nonetheless, KAVZ decked out its own pickup truck, complete with a mock transmitter consisting of two-by-fours covered in aluminum foil, and I sat in the back with my granddaughter broadcasting live, greeting the throngs of revelers who lined the parade route. And by throngs I mean tens. Maybe twenties. Shockingly, those folks had heard of KAVZ, and some of them shouted out, "Hey, Voice! How's it going, Voice! Good job, Voice!" Puzzled, I commented to our crew at parade's end, "Can you believe how many folks have heard of our radio station, and that we're known as 'Your Voice of the Valley'?"

They smiled and said, "They weren't talking about the radio station. They were talking about *you*. You are The Voice of the Valley."

Stunned and humbled, not knowing what to say or how to say it for once in my life, I whipped out a handkerchief, wiped my eyes, mumbled something about allergies, and made a quick exit.

I'm not going to tell you that Bucolia is a place where dreams can come true. But it is. Just trust me.

A couple of years, and several hundred hours of recorded pieces about everything from local concerts to cougar sightings to burn bans to thank-yous to underwriters to allegedly funny bits about cows and gardening later, since the current manager felt more comfortable serving behind the scenes, the folks at KAVZ figured they needed someone else to act as station manager.

Time for me to print up some new business cards.

Matthew Thuney

Chapter 15: Rocky

Rocky.

I may be wrong about this, and Lord knows it wouldn't be the first time (or the 1,271st), but I'm guessing that there aren't many human beings who can directly connect their spiritual awakening to a cat.

But that's my story, and as evidence I present the unquestionable fact that what follows is the most difficult chapter or segment or tale that I have ever written.

It had been a strange week, a wicked one really. The week of my 60th birthday. There were times in my life when I never ever thought I'd see sixty. Hell, there were times when I never thought I'd see thirty. But I did. Twice! Imagine that.

Several weeks before, I had received a request from our neighbors across the road—the best neighbors anyone could possibly ask for, and by then very close friends—to give the eulogy at the memorial of their son who had passed away suddenly and unexpectedly. Why, you may wonder, would they turn to me for such an honor? They had heard I was a pretty good writer, had heard that I had a history of public speaking, and had somehow found out that I had studied for the Episcopal ministry decades ago. Needless to say, I was indeed honored and humbly accepted their invitation.

To be perfectly honest, I had no earthly idea what to say about the untimely passing of their son. That kind of thing, well, it just seems like it ought not to happen. Ever.

But the mother wrote a wonderful account of her son's life. She provided the outline of words and thoughts, leading me down the trail toward finding her son's spirit and translating that spirit into words. But how to actually say those words, how to impart the essence of those life events and crystalline memories to a chapel full of bereft friends and relatives? People who had known this young man far more intimately and held him far more closely than I ever could have? Again, I had no earthly idea.

So, being a writer, I conjured up a web of words, wrapped it around the loving essence of what the young man's mother told me, then walked up to the podium at the front of the chapel and told the tale. I spoke the words, looking out over the sea of upturned faces. The mourners nodded knowingly at poignant remembrances, even chuckled at humorous vignettes. I stood up there and did my job. And I reckon I did it fairly well.

The family had requested a simple poem at the end—it was that one by Mary Frye, "Do Not Stand at My Grave and Weep." Short, eloquent. I launched into it with no small sense of pride, thinking "I've *got* this; I can *do* this." But I didn't and I couldn't. I began to break down. I lost my place. I looked down at the text. It had become oddly blurry. I gripped the podium. I dug my fingernails into the palms of my hands. Finally, semi-composed, I lifted my gaze to the assembled guests and declared in my folksiest manner, "Y'all are gonna have to help me with this." And somehow, I don't know how, they did. Their love cleared my eyes, and somehow, I don't know how, I finished the poem and felt the warmth of that room and those people rise up to Wherever that young man was.

How I got back to my seat without stumbling, tripping or collapsing completely, I don't quite recall. But that, as it turned out, was the beginning of my role as something of a bucolic cleric.

Now, back to the cat.

I love cats. I'm allergic to cats. Somehow, despite repeated trips to the doctor and one agonizing trip to an emergency room, I've never managed to link those two together in order to reach the logical conclusion that I should never have a cat.

Naturally, after dwelling in Bucolia for a couple of years, surrounded as I was by animals (some of the loathed bovine persuasion, some of the lovable canine persuasion, some of the curious coyote persuasion), I began fleetingly to wonder about acquiring a pet.

Although I was raised with beagles, I've never considered myself a dog person. Dogs can be hyperactive. Dogs can bark like mad. Dogs need lots of attention. Dogs can stink. Dogs can bite. And, let's face it, dogs are dumb. Now wait a minute, sure you can train dogs to perform basic tricks or tasks, but think about it. Would you call a human who can be easily trained to perform on command smart or dumb? See what I mean? (I'm assuming you said dumb, because otherwise you're a sadomasochist, tyrant, or both.) Dogs can be wonderful, loyal, delightful critters. *But...*

Cats? Cats are lovable but not needy. Cats sleep a lot. Cats purr. Cats are soft. Cats are warm. And, best of all, they poop where you ask them to.

So, when a stray momma cat gave birth to a litter of wild kitties underneath the building in town where I worked at the time, guess what? If you shouted out, "I'll bet you ended up with a kitten!" you'd be half-right. We ended up with two kittens.

Clearly, with my rampant allergies, two kittens was not the best of ideas. But I did bring them both home, because, well, they had to go somewhere, right?

To say that Donna was slightly taken aback at the sight of two kittens being delivered to our home by yours truly, the Allergic Wonder, would be akin to saying that Poland and France found the German blitzkrieg to be somewhat annoying. True, the playful balls of fur did somewhat soften her heart, but the rapidly developing spectacle of my reddening, itchy eyes, snifflerific runny nose, and wheezing gasps for air were simply too much for Donna to bear. Despite my groggy, antihistamine-garbled assurances of, "I'll be fide. Judst gib id a few dayds."

And then there was the problem of inter-kitty conspiracy. Being feral, these two shifty felines were not terribly fond of human company as yet. The result being that we rarely saw them. Except for the occasional mealtime dash, these two, a boy and a girl, were more like ghost cats. The food disappeared and so did they.

They would work together to find tricky places to hide. Under a bed, behind a couch, atop a kitchen cabinet, inside an unattended drawer, these kitties were tiny, wily, and extremely cunning. But we always managed to find them after diligent searching. Until one frightening day when Donna and I thought surely we had lost our two new furry charges.

We came home from work in town to a seemingly empty house. Resigned to our new post-homecoming ritual, we availed ourselves of the tools of the cat-finding trade, rounding up broom handles, yardsticks, flashlights, step stools, and ladders. We searched and searched, poked and prodded, high and low, but found no trace of our two shadowy co-conspirators.

Had they possibly somehow escaped? This was a new home, airtight, nary a gap nor hole to be found anywhere. Still, it being summer, we checked all the windows and made sure each screen was still intact. Nope, no escape routes there. Wandering around the house in a puzzled daze, Donna and I finally heard a faint rustle in one corner of the living room. Bizarrely, it seemed to be emanating from the pellet stove. Yet we'd already looked behind the pellet stove, six or seven times. On a whim, Donna bent down and peered into one of the side vents. She spied an unmistakable tuft of fur and what could possibly be a bit of tail. I peeked into another tiny crack. A tiny feline eye stared back at me.

How in the world has those kittens crammed themselves into such tiny metal confines? We still haven't quite figured that one out. Nonetheless, a wave of relief washed over us until two things sprung to mind: 1)how the heck were we going to extricate the cats, and 2) we sure as hell were glad it wasn't winter or, with our pellet stove hooked to an automatic thermostat switch, we might have come home to two cooked kitties.

Eventually, with Donna and her superior knees crouched in back of the stove and me handing her various screwdrivers and wrenches, we were able to remove the vents and the kitties after copious sweating and cursing. For days after that, various barriers were erected around the pellet stove in a vain attempt to keep the kittens from re-entering their metallic lair. Nothing seemed to work, and we must have disassembled and reassembled that doggone pellet stove five or six times, until finally a scheme was devised wherein virtually every towel and washcloth in the house was shoved into some nook or cranny so that the cats were forced to surrender and acknowledge that they just had to suck it up and hang out with these two implacable humans.

And to this day, that pellet stove makes odd and unsettling noises whenever it's on full blast, rumbling and vibrating like it's on the verge of liftoff for orbital velocity. No doubt we re-inserted some panel upside-down, or maybe left a serviette crammed in an unknown vent.

Still, it remained clear that, with my alarming consumption of Kleenex and Benadryl, combined with even greater incidences of incredibly loud sneezing attacks and more huffing and puffing than usual, something had to be done. I might survive one cat, but two?

These cats were boy and girl, and, frankly, I was more partial to the girl at first. But she boasted a much fuller coat than the boy, hence hosting more potential allergens. So a decision was made to find a good home for the girl. Which turned out to be easy, since several of my acquaintances at work in town offered to adopt the kitty and they all held the promise of good homes. But giving her away, I will readily admit, was not easy. Kittens can grow on you like zucchini on a vine.

So what, you may wonder, were these cats named? Well, Donna and I had toyed with names for the female but never come up with something suitable. I had, however, already named her brother.

The male kitty was a fighter from the get-go. He was hard to capture and cage, and even harder, when the time came, to transfer him from cage to carrier for the journey from town to Bucolia.

The task seemed simple enough: simply shuttle the kitten from the cage provided by the Humane Society into the carrier provided by yours truly. Jam one enclosure up against the other, open both doors, and wait until the cat in question waltzes right on through, right?

Well, this cat would have none of that. For one thing, the doors didn't quite line up. One opened from the top, the other from the side. This left a small gap between cage and carrier, and required that the two components be briefly separated in order to close the door on the captured kitty. Enlisting the assistance of Olive, a fellow worker and feisty grand-matron in her own right, we did indeed open both doors, quickly jam said enclosures together, and waited. The cat in the cage looked up at me in a rather sly and challenging way, as if to say, "What now, sport? What's your next move?" It became abundantly clear that his next move was *not* to move.

We had to force the issue, so Olive began to lift up the cage containing the kitty and sort of shove it towards the carrier on my end, as though she were pounding reluctant ketchup out of its unyielding bottle. As the angle twixt carrier and cage increased, along with the gap, I swear that cat almost winked at me, then made his move.

With lightning speed, he darted into that gap, banging his head on the cage and scampering behind a castle of boxes beneath a set of stairs. Olive hustled over to one side of the cat's stronghold, and I to the other. Surprised by our counter-attack, the furry dart headed straight toward me. Somehow—and my reflexes are about as fast as the aforementioned ketchup—I managed to grab hold of his midsection. Which this kitty did not appreciate. Not one bit.

He writhed, scratched, and clawed, but between the two of us Homo sapiens, we managed to wrangle the feline into the carrier, close the door, and commence to dressing my wounds. It wasn't until I got the kitty safely home that I noticed he, too, had sustained wounds. His attack against the cage door had resulted in a slight cut on his brow and a bloody nose.

Hence, "Rocky."

He would have made Sylvester Stallone proud.

After we ushered off Rocky's sister to her new home, an odd thing happened. Rocky ceased being a ghost cat. He began checking out his new home, his curiosity even extending to his new companions, Donna and I.

Then something even odder happened. Rocky gradually began to bond to me. After a couple of weeks, he simply couldn't seem to leave me alone. In some deep and mysterious way, we had become best buddies. He would follow me from room to room, always seem to be curious about what I might do next, and, when he needed a rest, paced around until I slumped into my recliner and then hopped up onto my lap.

An unexpected turn of events for a human allergic to cats and a cat who had been corralled by that human.

We even played a sort of hide-n-seek game together. Rocky would hunker down in our bathroom tub, then I would wander in pretending not to know where on earth he could be. Slowly, I would inch my way toward the tub, hunched over like a lurker, until my eyes cleared the tub's edge and met Rocky's eyes, which were always wide with surprise, as if to say, "How did you possibly find me here?" Then I'd leave, only to return a few minutes later, repeat the process,

162

and Rocky again would gaze at me with amazement, "Dang! Found me again! How do you do that?"

Occasionally, after a few post-dinner cocktails, I would change the game, using my outstretched hand instead of my head and eyes. Following several applications of Cortisone and Band-Aids, I learned not to do that anymore.

All through that winter, Rocky and I seemed inseparable. Donna and I began jokingly referring to Rocky as my daemon, a reference to a series of fantasy books by Philip Pullman. In his terrific trilogy entitled His Dark Materials, Pullman reached back into ancient mythology to create creatures—seemingly ordinary animals—who were metaphysically attached to his human characters. These daemons were said to be the physical manifestation of one's inner self, and a person forcibly separated from his or her daemon would suffer immense emotional and intellectual loss.

Sure enough, while away at work or running errands, I would miss my Rocky daemon and wonder what he might be up to. When he greeted me upon coming home, it was as though I were put back together, made whole again.

If I was the primary object of Rocky's affection, Donna seemed to be the primary object of his mischief. The most glaring example of that would be the Christmas tree battles.

I have always been a proponent of real Christmas trees, live or fresh-cut with that memorable holiday aroma and with branches and needles pointing every which-way. But—and this will likely come as a shock to no one—I turned out to be wildly allergic to evergreen conifers. In fact, my very first Christmas with Donna and her two kids (soon to be my step-children, although I completely consider them my own, much to their chagrin) was spent fully decorating and subsequently fully un-decorating a gorgeous tree that Donna's son David and I had spent the afternoon secretly selecting and chopping down as a surprise for Donna and daughter Rachel. That tree might as well have been a seven-foot-tall longhaired Himalayan cat. No sooner had we emptied three boxes of lights, garland, and balls onto the tree than my eyes puffed up, out came the Kleenex, down came the decorations, and out on the porch went the tree. A week later, once the allergens had dissipated, the lonely tree was allowed back into our home and re-dressed in its holiday attire.

So Donna and I were among the very few visitors to Christmas tree lots who requested not the freshest, but the oldest tree on the lot. We got a lot of funny looks.

You'll notice I employed the past tense there. Well, it took about 15 years and a move from town to country, but Donna, one of those blasphemous admirers of artificial trees, finally convinced me that it would involve much less hassle and work—not to mention being less expensive in the long run—to purchase a tree in a box. So that's what we did for our very first Christmas in Bucolia. Kind of ironic that we found it prudent to purchase an artificial tree once we were actually surrounded by real ones. But I must grudgingly admit that the doggone thing looks incredibly real and is perfectly proportioned. That tree is Donna's holiday baby. She takes child-like delight in decorating it each year; I'm not sure which is brighter, the stellar array of lights and multicolored ornaments or the beaming smile on Donna's face.

Hence, Donna did not take it kindly when, as Christmas time rolled around, Rocky was overjoyed to see that we had erected a giant climbing toy especially for him right there in our living room! Now he had a brand new hide-and-seek venue. We'd be strolling by the tree, notice a tell-tale shaking, and out would pop Rocky's whiskered mug from between the branches. I was greatly amused. Donna, not so much.

Especially when it came time to place her prized, delicate, expensive ornaments on said tree. As each decoration found its carefully selected spot, Donna would glare down at Rocky with a look that said, "Don't even think about it." Rocky, wide-eyed and tail switching back and forth in anticipation, was doubtless thinking, "Oh, this truly is amazing. First the climbing toy, and now all these shiny and dangly attachments for me to play with? Really, you shouldn't have…but thank you *so* much!"

So the battle was joined. Donna and I would be sitting quietly—me with a book, Donna with her cross-stitch—and we'd hear a Christmassy jingle-jangle emanating from the tree. A moment later, some sparkling object would bounce down the tree, falling from limb to limb to land softly on the (thankfully deep shag) carpet below. Rocky's excited face would emerge from the spot formerly occupied by the ornament, expecting praise and adulation for the wondrous task he had just completed.

However, the glare and accompanying, "*Rocky!!!*" issued forth by Donna did not bespeak praise and adulation. The flummoxed kitty must have figured he'd simply done it wrong, because he would immediately set about attacking his next gleaming victim from a different angle. Maybe *this* time he'd get it right.

And so it went throughout the holiday season: rustle, tinkle, bounce bounce bounce, clunk, shout, chuckle. The chuckle was, of course, my contribution. Surprised I didn't get a lump of coal in my stocking that year.

With the advent of spring, Rocky began showing a decided interest in what was happening outside our doors and windows. I just didn't have the heart to keep him indoors when there was so much to be experienced outdoors. Besides, the little guy had been born outdoors and spent the first few weeks of his life exploring the yard, parking lot, and alleyways at the workshop in town. Surely he would know how to fend for himself and where he'd need to return to for food, petting, and lap time.

So, little by little we let Rocky out to explore while Donna and I worked in the garden or relaxed on the deck. It was like watching a child take his first steps. He would cautiously slink out the front door; make his way gingerly down the stoop; tiptoe across the gravel walkway; then become simply overwhelmed by the plants, flowers, and insects. Wondering eyes wide and twitching Rocky nose working overtime, he would stop and thoroughly inspect every blade, leaf, and bud, rearing up from ground level only to bat his paws at some passing bumblebee or butterfly. Rocky reminded me of Ferdinand the bull in the classic children's story; not much of a fighter now, more content to stop and smell the flowers. And he would always check in with us, just to see what we were doing.

Rocky seemed right at home in Bucolia.

It was never a problem luring him back inside at the end of the day. Rocky would either follow us back through the door or come fairly quickly when we called his name.

Then one late afternoon, he didn't answer our call. Afternoon faded into evening, still no sign of my daemon. We searched with flashlights, called and called, but no Rocky. I began to feel sick. Not in my stomach, but somewhere near my heart. I hardly slept that night, tossing, turning, getting up frequently to peer outside. Nothing. Eventually, toward dawn, I conked out.

I was awakened a couple of hours later by a shout from Donna, who had wandered out onto the deck for an early morning cup of coffee. "Rocky!" she was shouting, only this time it was a happy shout. Rocky had found his way home, and he looked like...well, he looked like something the cat dragged in. Having just tumbled out of bed and made my way to the front door, I was shocked to see this jumbled mass of frazzled fur, caked in dust and dirt, with an exhausted, woeful and forlorn look in his eyes as if to say, "Well, I'm not doing *that* again." I was shocked, and ecstatic.

Rocky spent the next few days indoors, just sleeping, eating, and generally being your typical housecat. But we were soon to learn that you can give a feral cat a fine house and home but you'll be hard pressed to keep him from doing what he wants to do, and that is to roam.

A week or two later, Rocky began venturing outside again. I didn't like the idea, but somehow felt he had learned his lesson not to do *that* again. But he did do that again. Only this time, he did not come back.

Bucolia is indeed a marvelous and mysterious place. In the fostering of life, it can be ever so gentle. In the taking of life, savagely harsh.

I can't tell you how many days I spent wandering the property, calling out Rocky's name. I can't tell you because it all became a blur, just as my eyes are blurring now. One afternoon, a still, small voice inside me said simply, "It's enough. It's enough, and time for you to mourn." So I tucked a flask of scotch into my hip pocket and set off down the road toward a little wooded creek. There, I ducked into the underbrush and found a perfect log to perch on. Then I drank. And I cried. I drank. And I cried. I didn't really know how to say goodbye to my lovable little daemon, so I just wrote this:

Rocky

You came into our house, meek as a mouse,
And quickly hid in our stove.
The strands of my life, unbound by strife,
With love and great care you re-wove.
Then you disappeared, and all I had feared
Returned as my heart was undone.
I tried to re-start, fill the hole in my heart,
And now, of cats we have two.
I do love them dearly, but I know this clearly,
Neither of them, Rocky, is you.

Yes, it took two cats to take Rocky's place: Lord Neo the Haughty, and Karma the LoveBug. We adopted them, they adopted us, and those two are never, ever going outside. We're all happy together, the four of us *and* the Christmas tree. But still...
Call me a fool, call me maudlin, call me a capricious cat-lover who values feline life over human. I've been called worse, much worse, and frankly my dears, I don't give a damn. I know what I love, I know when it's gone, and I know I miss it.

Rocky touched me deeply. His passing tore a hole clean through my soul. Thank Whatever Is Holy that the bright side of Bucolia in all its daily glory is there to fill that hole that the dark side of Bucolia punched through. Where loss can slowly be mourned, love can quickly be celebrated. And forever.

Chapter 16: *The Pillar and the Dragonfly*

About three years after relocating to Bucolia, I received the shock of my life. And I've been shocked plenty. It's a wonder my hair isn't permanently standing on end.

It was a New Year's Eve. I remember that distinctly, because Donna and I were hosting our annual New Year's Eve party and prediction fest. It's a simple affair, just a few friends and neighbors. One stipulation is you have to be able and willing to attend. And by that I mean able to stagger home on foot afterward or willing to spend the night at our place.

Very low-key. Conversation, libation, and predictions for the coming year. At the following year's New Year's Eve gathering, we re-read said predictions and share a good laugh over their intoxicated incorrectness. If my Scotch-fueled visions had been accurate over the years, North and South America would have been rent entirely asunder by now with massive earthquakes, aliens would have revealed their Earthly presence to an astonished populous, and, wildest of all, the Seattle Mariners would have three or four World Series championships under their belt.

This particular year, I was asked to present our radio station's tech wizard Michael Gilbert, an amazing man of many talents who dedicated himself to keeping us on-air, with our valley's annual "Pillar of the Community" award. Without Michael, there would have been no "Voice of the Valley." The airwaves of Bucolia would have been silent as a mournful mime.

So, I prepared some witty words of wisdom and praise a few days in advance, and settled in with my friends and neighbors at Casa Bucolia; drinks in hand, tall tales at the ready, prognostications just waiting to wash over us, awaiting the dropping of the ball and popping of the cork. When the time came for me to mosey on down to our community hall, where a much more lively New Year's Eve celebration was in progress, I politely excused myself from my guests, gathered up my speaking notes, and followed Donna out to the car.

Donna's idea of exotic libation is a few glasses of Snapple or (when she really wants to walk on the wild side) a sip or two of sparkling cider. Donna doesn't drink much. Cheap date. One of the reasons I married her. But don't tell her I said so.

Donna chauffeured me down our windy road, over the rickety old one-lane bridge, across what passes for the local highway, to our beloved bucolic hall. The hall was packed with revelers, our local "house band" was rendering its customary impeccable versions of classic rock songs, and Jim Abernathy, probably the closest thing we've come to a community ombudsman (and a fellow volunteer at KAVZ) approached me with a smile.

"Oh good, you're here," said Jim, "I'll introduce you." Jim made his way to the stage as the band finished their song, shrugged out of their instruments, and took a much-needed break. After a few kind words of introduction, Jim motioned me to the nearest microphone, and I commenced to wax eloquent, lavish in my praise for Michael Gilbert and his incredibly generous technical support and sage advice regarding our struggling radio station.

The celebratory assemblage stood and applauded, Jim handed Michael his "Pillar of the Community" plaque, and Michael said a few touching words of thanks. I began inching my way off the stage, proud to have been able to contribute to the evening's festivities, eager to return to my guests and a hilarious night of laughter, companionship, and silly sooth-saying. What followed next was not a catastrophic seismic event in Argentina, an otherworldly encounter, or a walk-off home run by Edgar Martinez in the seventh game of the World Series. Nonetheless, I certainly would never have predicted it.

As I attempted to make good my escape, Jim grabbed my arm. "You're not going anywhere," he laughed, dragging me back to a microphone. He addressed the crowd, saying something about, "Our second 'Pillar of the Community award," and launched into a discourse about someone else who had also given a great deal to the local area and deserved the community's thanks and recognition. Next thing I knew, Jim was thrusting another plaque toward me. It had my name on it.

I haven't the vaguest idea what I said in acknowledgment of this wildly unexpected honor. I only hope it was somewhat intelligible and devoid of gratuitous profanity. The next thing I do remember is receiving numerous handshakes and pats on the back while exiting the hall, then sitting in the car with this weird and wonderful framed document in my lap.

Then I was home with my friends, who delighted in opining that surely there had been a misprint, and the correct version of the award should read "*Pillow* of the Community." Although it's unlikely that a pillow big enough for my head at that point in time could possibly exist. Still, I gallantly withstood the barrage of deprecating comments, smiling all the time and enjoying every minute of it.

But the truth of the matter is that Bucolia is my pillar, not the other way around. This tiny community tucked far away from the hustle and bustle, the confusing discord of life lived in convenient but close confines, has supported me in ways too numerous to mention and too deep to divine.

All that I had left behind in my previous life, I rediscovered here. Especially the cornerstones, pillars if you will, of my personal core. You might call them the three R's: writing, radio, religion. Okay, so that's two R's and a W; you get the gist.

Bucolia helped me become reacquainted with my journalistic muse. I had become bogged down in the quagmire of political punditry, issuing forth diatribes about this or that issue or cause. Impassioned? Yes, but a far cry from my roots, when I started out by regaling readers with allegedly witty tales about my personal, business, and family life. Folks really seemed to get a kick out of that. But after I picked up the political bullhorn and began shouting about equality, justice, compassion, cooperation? Well, some folks liked that, too. It was just too darn loud for many, though. And now, look, here I am back to storytelling. Here's hoping you feel properly regaled.

Bucolia gave me the gift of a radio voice, too. Without that small band of crazed community volunteers who transformed the extremely lofty and highly unlikely goal of building a radio station into a beaming, streaming reality, I'd probably be growling into my laptop microphone right now pretending to be a some crazed liberal bastion of punditry. No one in their right mind wants to hear that. Nor in their left mind. Honestly.

When it comes to religion, I'm not talking about churches and bibles, hymns and collection plates. I'm talking about the fields and the animals that roam them; the skies and the birds that sail there; the far-flung houses and the folks who tread their floors, tend their hearths, gaze out their windows, and watch it all play out in a sublime four-part seasonal symphony of life and love. We all mourn and celebrate together, and that's my church now. Bucolia humbles me and gives me strength, touches my soul and makes my heart soar like a hawk. If that isn't the essence of grace, then I don't know what is. And for that gift of grace, I will be eternally thankful.

Yes, thankful even for the cows. Especially Enrique.

Bucolia is my pillar, and I am overcome by its support.

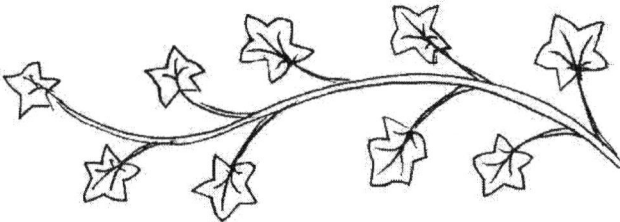

Often on a hot, hushed summer day, I'll find myself standing in a field or sitting in a garden. Just soaking in the warmth of the sun, the complete stillness of the languid afternoon, with nothing particular on my mind. All of a sudden, nature will come to life all around me: buzzing bees, flitting hummingbirds, fluttering butterflies. Sometimes life comes at you that way, all in a bothersome flurry. Might sting you, might not. Might startle you, might amaze you. Most likely will just plain confuse you. Caught by surprise, your first inclination might be to bat it away. Life can be annoying when you don't expect it. And you can forget about life leaving you alone.

But every now and then when I'm just outdoors, just being out in the open, just being alive on a hot, hushed summer day, a dragonfly will come along. A dragonfly will generally zip around in fits and starts, checking you out before it decides how to proceed. Sometimes it'll circle you in a jagged dance of curiosity and assessment. Then a dragonfly makes its choice: it'll either move on to the next subject of exploration, or it will stop right in front of you and look you straight in the eye.

When that happens—when you're eye to eye with a dragonfly— magic occurs. A connection is made, a bridge appears, and if you listen very carefully you just might hear the universe say, "Here am I, all around you. The beauty, the mystery, the challenge of everything that is. Will you take it all in; embrace every fleeting second, every chance encounter? Will you allow it all to come together and weave your life? If so, step right this way."

It's a bridge anyone can fit through. Though I reckon you might be able to make it over the mountain instead. It'll just take a little longer.

Welcome to Bucolia.

ABOUT THE AUTHOR

Matthew wrote his first book, *The Egg*, when he was five years old. That is, if you can call a disjointed ten-page ramble about a mother dinosaur in search of her baby son (somehow attacking and sacking Chicago in the process) a book. Undeterred, he's been writing ever since. The past 30 years or so have seen Matthew scribbling humor and human-interest pieces and crafting political blogs for consumption in the Pacific Northwest.

Besides the printed word, he has also shared a long-standing love affair with radio. In fact, he even attended the Columbia School of Broadcasting in San Francisco. While he truly enjoyed writing news copy and coming up with funny on-air segments, Matthew just didn't have the gift of gab back then to keep up the requisite DJ patter. Spiritually, Matthew has always been a student and seeker. Early on, it looked as though his path would lead to the Episcopal ministry. Luckily for the Episcopal Church, that path turned into a 40-year detour. But everything started falling into place when Matthew and his wife moved to the hinterlands of northwest Washington. Lo and behold, he rediscovered his journalistic muse, reporting on his bumbling attempts to adapt to country living. He rediscovered his radio voice when a small band of crazed volunteers fired up a community radio station. And he rediscovered his spiritual roots as new friends and neighbors approached Matthew to give eulogies and even preside over the marriages of loved ones.

Who'da thunk it?

Certainly not his long-suffering spouse, who thankfully remains at his side. Nor their puzzled families, who long ago gave up trying to figure Matthew out. Nor their two-and-a-half cats, who are always giving him quizzical looks that seem to say, "What the heck are you up to now?" or "Where's the treats?" or "Will you sit down already--I need a lap."

ABOUT THE ILLUSTRATOR

In her formative years, Ellen studied fine art and business at the University of Utah, attended the Salt Lake Academy of Graphic and Fine Arts and attended Successful Artist School. She has more recently taken courses at Western Washington University, Shoreline College and accomplished Teaching Artist Training through the Washington State Arts Commission. For personal growth, she has a CTM through Toastmasters International and is a graduate of Excellence Northwest.

Always interested in the evolutionary trail of life, Ellen has been a fashion illustrator for a sporting goods company, cartographer for an engineering firm, product illustrator and copywriter for a nationwide drugstore, manager for several photography labs, and graphic designer for various ad agencies.

Recent work includes creating sequential art for stories and books, painting public murals, being lead scenic painter for a 1500 seat theatre, teaching art to children and adults and having an annual commission to festively paint the featured window at Bellingham's Cruise terminal.

She has been influenced by such artists as Peter Max, Maxfield Parrish, Vincent van Gogh, Auguste Rodin, Leonardo de Vinci and Buonarroti Michelangelo.

Made in the USA
Las Vegas, NV
27 April 2021